HOPE
for ECONOMIC HOPELESSNESS

HOPE

for ECONOMIC HOPELESSNESS

Your Hand Up, **Not** Hand Out

BRIG HART

Renowned Micro-Entrepreneurship Expert

with **Billy Glynn**

HOPE FOR ECONOMIC HOPELESSNESS

Copyright © 2012 by Brig Hart

Published by
ISB Publishing
2128 Boll Street
Dallas, TX 75024 USA

ISBN 978-1-9377-1708-7

Printed in the United States of America
10 9 8 7 6 5 4 3 2 1

All hard work brings a profit,
but mere talk leads only to poverty.
Proverbs 14:23

TABLE OF CONTENTS

THE WORLD WE LIVE IN 9

Hopelessness is a Dangerous Job 12

Capitalism: A Hand Up vs. Socialism: A Hand Out 16

Debt vs. Deficit. 21

Change the Equation 26

Is There an Immediate Solution? 27

Zero 28

The Power of Hope 30

Hopeless but not Helpless 31

MICRO ENTREPRENEURSHIP: THE INDUSTRY 33

There is Only Safety in Numbers 34

The Industry Has Grown Up 37

Going Pro 37

Taking the Industry to New Heights 38

Influence 42

SOLUTIONS THAT CAN DRIVE THE INDUSTRY TO NEW HEIGHTS. 45

License and Registration 45

Standards Body 49

Code of Conduct 49

The Distributor's 10 Commandments. 50

The Company — Micro Entrepreneur Bond 53

Multi Branding 55

WHAT CAN MICRO ENTREPRENEURSHIP DO FOR YOU..................57

Success is not a Destination it is a Journey............. 57
Micro Entrepreneurship Motivates Positive Behavior... 58
  Purpose.. 59
  Recognition...................................... 60
  Work 60
  Money.. 61
  Rewards 61

YOU HAVE THE POWER TO CHANGE 63

The Power of Ones.................................. 63
There Can Be No Success without U 64
Everyone knows somebody who will.... My Story....... 65
You are the Key 73
The Rat Race....................................... 75
What Can You Do Right Now.......................... 77
Others Will Support You 78
Let's Go Fishing 78
I Am All In 81

ONE STEP AT A TIME...85

  Walk First...................................... 85
  Pick up the Pace................................ 86
  Gidee Up! 86

BASIC TRAINING 91
How You Make Money 91
Binary Compensation Plan 92
Unilevel Compensation Plan 93
Hybrid Compensation Plan 93
Direct selling 101 94
Direct Selling 102 96
Strong or Weak 96
Direct Selling 103 101
Walking the Walk 101
Direct Selling 104 104
The Basic System of Success 105
Direct Selling 105 108
Failure is not an Option 113

GETTING PERSONAL 117
Life 101 117
Life 102 120
It Starts with Today 120
Life 103 122
Life 104 124
I am Positive 125
Life 105 126

WHY NOT YOU, WHY NOT NOW 131
Take Action 133

WORKS CITED 137

APPENDIX A 139

APPENDIX B 151

APPENDIX C 153

ABOUT THE AUTHORS 154

THE WORLD WE LIVE IN

There are 7 billion people on earth and only approximately 1.2 billion jobs. According to a recent book, *The Coming Jobs War*, by Jim Clifton, CEO of Gallup, there are 3 billion people on earth that simply want a good job and that means 1.8 billion people won't get one. The math just doesn't work, and for over 1 billion people it never will. They won't find a good job or they will simply never have a job and tens of millions join their ranks every year. This is an underlying issue that affects all humanity and the scale of the related issues are simply overwhelming.

- Almost half the world — over 3 billion people — live on less than $2.50 a day. [1]
- At least 80% of humanity lives on less than $10 a day. [2]
- According to UNICEF nearly a billion people entered the 21st century unable to read a book or sign their names and two thirds of them are women. And they will live, as now, in more desperate poverty and poorer health than those who can. [3]
- Some 1.1 billion people in developing countries have inadequate access to water, and 2.6 billion people lack basic sanitation. [4]
- 1.6 billion people — a quarter of humanity — live without electricity. [5]
- A UNICEF study done in 2005 shows, 1 billion children live in poverty (1 in 2 children in the world). 640 million live without adequate shelter, 400 million have no access to safe water, 270 million have no access to health services. 10.6 million died in 2003 before they reached the age of five (or roughly 29,000 children per day). [6]

- Less than one percent of what the world spends every year on weapons was needed to put every child into school by the year 2000 and yet it did not happen. [7]

Those are just a few of the statistics and only the tip of the iceberg that is melting. They have grown over the past five to ten years and continue to grow each day a solution is not found.

Now, just imagine all those people and their feeling of hopelessness, knowing they will never be able to improve their lives and the lives of their family, that whatever they are doing now is all there is. It is far more pervasive than you think across Africa, India, China, Mexico, Brazil, Russia, and Europe. In the United States, the statistics are broadcast to the world on the news every day. Joblessness and hopelessness are right around the corner regardless of where you live on the planet.

Just in America, there is historic unemployment, underemployment and an already mature and growing permanent social underclass. Added to the staggering numbers of those without jobs across the world, are the tens of millions of college graduates who can't find a job and aren't even included in those numbers. Also not counted, are the millions of others who were never employed, or do not collect unemployment, or are no longer looking for anything but a government bailout. These vast numbers are conveniently left out of the statistics.

The fact is more than half the world has become part of the same permanent social underclass I am describing, according to a World Bank report in 2008. [1] They have little — and most have no — hope of ever graduating into ranks of even the lower middle class. Tomorrow for them is more of the same poverty, hopelessness and lack of basic human needs. They simply wish for something more than they have today. Most want a hand up not a hand out. These issues are at the root of many of the world's problems.

Joblessness is not just an economic or political hazard contained within any one country's borders. Each country's problems now impact the world's social and economic systems. The systems are interwoven so tightly that any disruption can cause the web to rattle and fall apart. The revolution in Libya caused worldwide oil price hikes affecting the global economy. Iran, Iraq, Egypt and others have caused acute havoc in the financial and energy markets. The US and Europe almost brought down the entire global system. Japan's Tsunami was felt around the world. The massive debt of many western nations is keeping the world back on its heels, just needing a small push to put us over the edge.

Jobs are the underpinnings of any nation's economy. Without jobs there is not enough money to collect in taxes from the income earned and less money in the pockets of its citizens to generate adequate consumption to sustain any economy. Therefore, jobs, or rather the lack of them, is one of the greatest risks to global security and stability. Even with approximately one hundred trillion dollars of new economic favor expected to rain down on the world over the next 50 years, jobs will always be outstripped by population growth. The numbers will always be growing further into the red.

In other growth periods, like the "baby boomer" generation in the United States, jobs were plentiful and were in line with the number of people looking for them. This is has not been the case for a long time, is not the case now, and will not be in the future. Jobs cannot be created fast enough. Even in China and India hundreds of millions have risen into the ranks of the middle class over the past few decades but even those booming economies have left tens of millions behind.

The world simply cannot keep up the economic pace of the past several decades, as more and more people need work and practically all economies have almost reached their maximums. This is true in almost every modern nation and far worse in the poorer, "Third World" nations. There is presently no way out.

Hopelessness is a Dangerous Job

The overthrow of the Egyptian government is a prime example of how dangerous and unstable a society can become without economic hope and viability. The Arab Spring took root in Tunisia and quickly spread to Egypt. It began in Egypt for reasons many people are not aware of. Few jobs and soaring food prices were the underlying cause of the revolt that led to the overthrow of Mubarak's government. Hope for a better future and economic prosperity have now faded into the background. With even fewer jobs than before, Spring has turned to Winter. An article that appeared in *Bloomberg Business Week* on March 28, 2012, "Arab Spring Turns Economic Winter on More Joblessness", focuses directly on this issue. Egyptians wanted to be free to pursue their own form of happiness and to find a way out of merely surviving day in and day out.

Waleed Rashed is one of the founders of the non-violent April 6, Movement which started in 2008. He led a call for massive demonstrations on Police Day, January 25, 2011 and together with other youth movements, organized the 18-day peaceful uprising that culminated in President Hosni Mubarak's departure on February 11, 2011. Once it began it caused a firestorm that shook the nation. It was not Social Media that fueled the fires in Egypt, as we were led to believe, or Google that brought people pouring into the streets. The personal revolution that the people of Egypt already had within them is what compelled them to demand change.

We interviewed Waleed for this book to hear his experience firsthand. He was quick to point out that 40% of Egyptians live under the poverty line according to the World Bank standards. Even those with jobs were not making enough money to afford a decent lifestyle. There was economic hopelessness, poverty and "the people had nothing to lose". He explained that the uprising began long before the demonstrations took place. It was the "revolution inside" that was already burning in the hearts and minds of the people; all that was needed was a spark.

Waleed pointed out that he was not alone in the path to revolution in Egypt. He, like his heroes; Rosa Parks, Gandhi, Martin Luther King, Mandela and Lech Walesa, also became a spark for freedom. Like Waleed, some people will act on creating change. Others will watch and wait. The world seems to be watching and waiting for its own jobs revolution and I believe Micro Entrepreneurship is the spark that can ignite it.

According to Waleed, everyone has the capability to act with courage. He wanted the readers to know if you think you would have avoided the risks he and his fellow activists faced, you only need to, "Imagine a life without freedom. Then the fire of the revolution inside burns brighter, stronger and with more force." Imagine a life without that change you seek — THEN — the revolution inside ignites. The revolution inside is waiting for you to act with courage.

My question remains; does the world have the courage to change the course we are on?

Even though a dictator had been removed, no new jobs arrived. As nations transition, violently or democratically, to new governments, there comes a fleeting sense of hope. Trading one form of government for another without economic changes and revitalization does not change fundamental issues; it temporarily masks the real problem. The hope that change brings, quickly turns into resentment and greater unrest if there are not enough jobs to fulfill the promise of a better day. Without a way to improve their lives, afford a decent living and have a sense of purpose chaos and violence will continue. Each instance of unrest threatens us all.

In a recent interview with *Forbes*, Jim Clifton presented a pointed view of what it means to have a job. "Gallup has discovered that having a good job is now the great global dream; it's the number one social value for everyone. This is one of our most powerful findings ever. A good job is more important than having a family, more compelling than democracy and freedom, religion, peace and so on. Those are all very important but they are now subordinate to the almighty good job. So it follows that everything turns on delivering this ultimate need. Stimulating job growth is the new currency of all leaders because if you don't deliver on it you will experience instability, brain drain, sometimes revolution — all of the worst outcomes of failed leadership. At the very least you will have no followers and no chance of re-election." [8]

This is a new dynamic that has been thrown onto the world stage. It is not that most people do not want to improve themselves; it is that they do not have the opportunity to do so. This attacks their self-esteem, self-worth and, worst of all, hope for brighter days to come. A black cloud looms over their dreams and will not go away unless something radical is done to change the course we are on. This problem is setting up entire societies for failure and more governments to potentially collapse under the weight of government debt being used to artificially subsidize their citizens and economies.

The toppling of a government in a modern nation like Egypt would be unthinkable even a decade ago. But to make matters worse, the Middle East has the largest unemployment rate in the world for its youth according to a report issued by the International Labour Office. [9] This demographic is critical to stabilize. Typically, when the younger population becomes disenchanted with government, they are far more likely to actively participate in demonstrations, violence and upheaval. Already in turmoil, the current and rising unemployment is sure to exasperate the issues that are wide spread throughout the Middle East and North African region.

The toppling of multiple nations' governments in the Middle East should paint a vivid picture of what is to come for many countries if economic hopelessness isn't resolved. This should not be taken lightly and roll across people's eyes while watching the events unfold on TV and the Internet. These nations have several of the largest standing armies on earth and remain unstable. Instability will persists if their economies don't satiate the masses or a new form of business building isn't created.

This has far reaching implications not only to stability in the region but collateral damage around the world. This is how wars begin and thus far it has been wars inside the countries among their population as we are now seeing in Syria and have witnessed in Libya. Tunisia and Yemen have joined the list of governments already overthrown in the region. It is a powder keg regardless of regime change and there are dozens of countries that have the same fundamental issues facing them around the world.

Wherever there is hopelessness that pervades a population, or lack of fulfillment of any basic need like food or water, there will be eventual upheaval or temporary containment through control by the harshest of dictator regimes. North Korea is racing down this path now and so is Pakistan, two nations with populations that are starving — starving for change and starving for something more than they have. They are potentially the future failing nations; it is just a matter of time. The most troublesome part is both countries have nuclear weapons. It is not just economic hopelessness and Maslow's hierarchy of needs not being fulfilled across the world; it is the time in human history where we must come up with larger and more scalable solutions to survive ourselves.

It is well documented, that the foremost measure of the stability of a country is the size and health of their middle class. If the vast majority of the world is trapped in an underclass while only small percentages graduate to even the lowest of middle class ranks, then the whole world is a time bomb. Many parts have started to explode already. We are just watching the previews in the Middle East. The movie hasn't even started yet.

Capitalism: A Hand Up vs. Socialism: A Hand Out

We saw what happened with the US housing crisis. It brought the whole world to its knees. This was just one industry. This was not the country or even one of its big states. It affected other industries and nations, but few take to heart that the entire global economic system could have collapsed. Our way of life in modern human history was inches away from being changed forever.

America is at the heart of the global economy and if it is sick then everyone is. This is why it is so important to understand the issues the United States faces as we discuss jobs and the state of affairs of the world. This comes down to the success of free markets and jobs compared with the cost of government subsiding jobs and their populations. It comes down to a hand up or hand out!

In America during the 1950's and 1960's a large percentage of people were self-employed and many of the entitlement programs that exist today were not even created yet. There are more food stamps, unemployment benefits and entitlement programs than ever before. For example, a record of approximately 44.7 million, 17 percent of the people in America, live in households that are receiving food stamps according to Department of Agriculture compared with 3 million in 1969. [10] In 2011, 46 million or 15% of the US population lived in poverty according to a report issues by the US Census Bureau in 2010. [11] Since the 50's and 60's the percentage of the population that is self-employed has plummeted. [12] More dependency, less jobs and more handouts is the last thing we need for the world. Micro Entrepreneurship is the answer, not more government spending to cover up the real cancer — lack of jobs.

With fewer jobs, there is much less disposable cash in the pockets of its citizens and consumption suffers greatly. This is the same for the rest of the world too. Without the revenue coming from taxes, the government has to borrow and borrow more to support itself. But instead of cutting back, more social programs are being created and more spending is happening and talk of more taxes is heard every day. This is a perfect storm that the US has created for itself and one Europe has already shown doesn't work.

In America, soaring gas prices, taxes on income at the federal and most state levels, taxes on cell phone usage, utilities, food, gas and everything its citizens buy in stores are just a few of the things left out when we hear about tax brackets. The total tax paid by every citizen is much more than what the US Federal Government is levying on its citizen's income on April 15th and little attention is paid to the cumulative taxes paid. Regardless of the amount of tax levied, this equation does not work. Europe has tried this for years and has even imposed a VAT (Value Added Tax) that applies to only consumers on top of the already over burdensome taxes levied. Less money in the consumer's pockets and more expensive products = disaster for any economy.

Let's take a look at just where the average US household spends their money if they are fortunate enough to have a job at all. According to the Bureau of Labor Statistics in 2010 the average income for a household in the US was over $62,000. Here is a breakdown [13]:

Income Before Taxes	$62,481	
Total Expenditures	$48,109	77%
Food	$6,129	10%
Housing	$16,557	26%
Apparel	$1,700	3%
Transportation	$7,677	12%
Healthcare	$3,157	5%
Entertainment	$2,504	4%
Cash Contributions	$1,633	3%
Personal Insurance / Pensions	$5,373	9%
Other	$3,379	5%

It looks like the average American family is doing ok, spending only about 77% of their money. That must mean each household is able to save over $14,000 a year; money to save for college for their kids, for a vacation, for retirement, or just for a rainy day.

But wait. Let's read that again, it is income before taxes. The Heritage Foundation estimates that in 2010 each household was taxed on average, $18,400 [14]. The taxes paid by each household makes the actual total expenditure higher by 10%, 15%, 20% and most more, depending on what tax bracket the family falls into, does not include State and Local Taxes, pages and pages of other taxes and most of the after tax expenditures are taxed again when purchased; food, clothing, transportation and more. The list of what Americans are taxed on each year is long and frightening.

Each year, on average, families are going into more and more debt or reaching out to the government for assistance or now having to cut back on expenditures to just get by. Every day more and more freedom is lost. That sounds more like the catch 22 that Main Street America is trapped in and the necessary reduction in household consumption puts America into the same position. It is no different around the world no matter what tax system, form of government or income earned, if any, the permanent social under class grows bigger and bigger while what is lauded about the middle class is not an accurate portrayal of the situation. (See Appendix C for a worksheet that will help you understand what position you find yourself in).

In America, the richest 10% pays 70% of the taxes and the top 50% pay 98% according to 2009 IRS data. [15] This is not incentivizing the job creators to create new jobs. It is redistribution of wealth at its very core. On top of that, the US is one of the highest tax nations on earth for corporations. This makes the US financial and employment markets unsavory at best, so other nations with much more business friendly environments are sucking the blood out of America's economy. America trails closely behind in corporate taxes, an already technically bankrupt nation, Japan whose debt to GDP ratio is 208% according to a CIA report and that ranks them #2 in the world, below only Zimbabwe. [16]

Like Europe, the United States, the most successful capitalistic society in history, has turned into an entitlement society with no means to sustain itself except through borrowing. Half of its citizens do not pay taxes at all according to a 2011 report from the Tax Policy Center [17] and one out of three of its citizens is receiving one form or another of government assistance. Historic unemployment isn't going away, it will only get worse and the statistics are just not a true measure of the real size of the problem.

According to an article that appeared in the USA Today in 2011, America has over $60 Trillion dollars of liabilities facing it in order to continue its entitlements over the next several decades. There are many other IOUs, too, and unlike a corporation that would have to report these massive obligations, the US government does not recognize them in their accounting until the checks are written. Therefore, if America were a company it would be illiquid, bankrupt and taken over by foreign nations and the whole modern world would come to an immediate halt. The following are some of the major programs and note the insurmountable social program obligations.

- Medicare: $24.8 trillion
- Social Security: $21.4 trillion
- Federal debt: $15 trillion
- Military retirement/disability benefits: $3.6 trillion
- Federal employee retirement benefits: $2 trillion
- State, local government obligations: $5.2 trillion

The debt as of the writing of this book is $15.6 trillion. By the time you read this it may be $16 trillion or more. Please go to (www.usdebtclock.org) and just see what a snapshot of what inevitability looks like.

There is more bad news. America's social programs are drained of cash even though its citizens have to mandatorily pay into those programs. According to a study done by The Congressional Research Service Social Security, Medicaid, Medicare and others programs now hold large amounts of government IOUs because the cash has been used for other spending.[18] State governments with large social programs are already technically bankrupt or close to the edge. Like the Federal Government, it is largely due to funding entitlements and rich benefits to public employees. They too are forced to keep borrowing money to prop up their people and government operations.

Debt vs. Deficit

The Federal Debt in America is always masked with word "deficit." The deficit is the amount of money the US, if it were a company, would be losing each year. That means the national debt has to be increased, so more and more borrowing has to occur to make up for it. If America was a company and had a $1 trillion deficit it would mean the company lost $1 trillion and in order to keep afloat it would have to borrow at least $1 trillion more just to operate. This over-spending and revenue under-performance has persisted for decades, except now it is expanding at an alarming rate. There has been more debt added to the US balance sheet in just the last three years than ever in history. This is not a Democrat or Republican or Independent issue, this is an American issue and the entire world's issue too. But at the root it is a jobs issue.

All this is just what we are being told. We surely do not know the whole picture. In fact, we know very little of the actual scale because we depend on the numbers we are fed. But the numbers do not lie. If tax revenues do not escalate and spending on entitlements is not reduced by large percentages, the house of cards will topple and that would wipe out the world economy. No amount of jobs on earth would save us.

In America, Europe and many other countries that are now more socialist than capitalist, the answer is taxing the rich. That is definitely not the answer. The only way out is to graduate large under-employed segments of the population, untether them from government dependency and transition them into more economically independent citizens.

Various authors over time have been credited for witting about the fall of the Athenian Republic some 2000 years ago. There is some confusion as to who contributed mutually or independently but there is an often quoted viewpoint, with an unclear source, that nonetheless, mirrors what is happening today. "A democracy is always temporary in nature; it simply cannot exist as a permanent form of government. A democracy will continue to exist up until the time that voters discover that they can vote themselves generous gifts from the public treasury. From that moment on, the majority always votes for the candidates who promise the most benefits from the public treasury, with the result that every democracy will finally collapse over loose fiscal policy, (which is) always followed by a dictatorship.

"The average age of the world's greatest civilizations from the beginning of history, has been about 200 years. During those 200 years, these nations always progressed through the following sequence:

From bondage to spiritual faith;

From spiritual faith to great courage;

From courage to liberty;

From liberty to abundance;

From abundance to complacency;

From complacency to apathy;

From apathy to dependence;

From dependence back into bondage."

That is prophetic to say the least. Much of the world is beyond apathy now and more than half of America alone is in dependency. The bondage is debt and the chains are that are holding prosperity back are primarily jobs. What is the solution — the Federal Reserve printing more money? Borrowing to provide unemployment benefits for over three years now? Bailouts and nationalizing entire industries, the new "HealthCaid" debacle, otherwise known as Obamacare, and soon bailing out entire states definitely are not. Where and when will it end? When will all this erupt? It ends the day any nation on earth holding US debt decides not to show up at the next treasury auction or decides to sell off large portions of the debt they own. That is when America runs into the brick wall and its biggest national security threat becomes reality.

If you think this is wrong just use a modern "democracy" like Greece as predictor.

Greece, one of the world's average economies, #41 According to a 2012 Central Intelligence Agency report, [19] caused global upheaval in the financial markets and social unrest in their streets by virtually collapsing under the weight of trying to subsidize their population and too many overpaid government jobs. The government tried to prop up its economy with a socialist strategy of handouts not hand ups. The country's citizens had become largely dependent on its government for their financial sustenance.

As people depend more and more on governments for their needs their freedom is slowly lost. How free are Americans, Europeans and many other countries when the majority of their citizens are under the crushing weight of debt and taxes and beholden to the government? Does not sound like freedom at all. In fact, today Greece's Economic Freedom Score is 55.4 making its economy the 119th freest in the 2012 index published by the Heritage Foundation. [20] That means it is a heavily social entitlement society and you see where that got them.

*"Government big enough to supply everything you
need is big enough to take everything you have ...
The course of history shows that as a government
grows, liberty decreases."*
—Gerald Ford, 1974, 38th President

Greece basically did go bankrupt. Except for a structured bail out by the European Economic Union the country would have had to declare bankruptcy. New austerity measures were forced upon them and their ability to borrow to keep their country from collapsing was close to being cut off. Even if confidence was restored so they could borrow more their rating was downgraded severely and the interest alone on its debt became too expensive regardless for Greece to save itself from itself. The country was forced to cut back on its social programs and riots broke out. People could no longer depend on the government for rich entitlements and jobs, now it is in dire need of a business model to solve its issues or this economic problem will persist.

The biggest problem of all is that this is happening in many countries simultaneously. The whole world is infected with the "lack of jobs disease," yet only the symptoms are being treated. It is like a putting a band aid on a severed limb. The band aids are governments trying to prop up their populations. They have been doing it for decades and now find themselves in financial trouble. In fact, the global employment crisis may as well be mummified for all the band aids wrapped around the issue for so many years. But there comes a time where quick fixes, governments and even capitalism can't come to the rescue anymore. That time unfortunately is now.

Change the Equation

The US AAA rating was downgraded by Standards & Poor's rating agency to AA+ in 2011. For the first time in history, the US lost its coveted premier rating status. In Europe, Ireland's booming economy came to a screeching halt when it too had to be bailed out with hundreds of billions from the European Union and other European nations are still on the brink. This is happening right before our eyes.

Entitlement societies and socialism do not work. Even with historic government assistance, worldwide hopelessness and economic sustainability have not been cured. The US itself cannot pay its debts without borrowing and rolling over payments, even on the interest, and neither can some of her state governments. The banks and insurance companies tried this roll over strategy with asset backed securities and mortgages and it almost collapsed modern society. The fundamental equation is simple. No jobs = No tax revenue. It is clear that fiscal policies and massive spending to fix the global jobs and economic issues are not working. Time has run out on the debt clock and we all know it. The US is borrowing just to keep its creditors from walking away from the table and toppling the economy. The only way out is for a transformational strategy that can propel millions of people into the ranks of being tax payers instead of tax collectors.

To make matters worse, taxes are one of the primary reasons companies are unwilling to create the jobs America needs to dig itself out of its own grave. Why would companies create domestic jobs if products could be manufactured more cheaply and services offered at lower costs with frankly, the same or even better quality than can be produced in the United States. This is a failed economic strategy.

Tax more and have even less jobs and still keep borrowing to make up the difference. Do the math. You will find it is mathematically impossible to avoid catastrophe this way. More taxing at this point can never pay off America's debt or the debts of many countries around the world. Unless something radically changes and something massive is done economically, politically and socially America will fast become the worst investment anyone in the world could make.

What if California, the world's 8th largest economy and already technically bankrupt; New York, the world's 16th largest economy; Italy; Portugal or worse the entire United States finds itself in the same position? Global chaos at a minimum would occur almost overnight. Without a robust economy worldwide, the whole thing collapses on itself and so would our way of life. Even if there was a massive economic comeback the population has grown so much over the last 10 years that a jobs-resurgence simply won't be enough. The simple math of population growth and job availability gets much worse. 1.8 billion will turn into 2 billion and 2.5 billion and so forth.

Is There an Immediate Solution?

The answer is yes and no. Micro Entrepreneurship has been prospering through direct selling for over 100 years. The number of entrepreneurs that make their living this way has swelled over the past 50 years and can grow larger and faster if the right conditions are set. It is not a cure-all for all the world's economic woes, or America's, but can have a blast radius substantial enough to do a lot of damage to the issue. Micro Entrepreneurship is much like becoming a mini-franchise owner that sells products goods or services. However, even with help from friendly governments it is not a panacea, but it is a big shot in the arm. Micro

Entrepreneurship can thrive but the right legal, regulatory and economic conditions still need to be in place to help it do so. That is why there must be a compelling government fiscal plan to unite it with. I feel a duty to offer some ideas on this issue, albeit not directly related to Micro Entrepreneurship. Someone has to do something, sometime soon. Since America is at the heart of the world's economy and in desperate need of good ideas, I offer the following. This book, after all, is about solutions.

Zero

My co-author, Billy Glynn and I call it 0-0-0. Billy has had almost 100 media appearances in the last three years, is the Author of The United States of Bankruptcy, and has been consistently prophetic according to the media hosts regarding the economy and social issues. He lives just a few doors from Herman Cain in Atlanta who ran for President in 2011 with a plan know as 9-9-9, so our plan is a bit poetic.

The plan calls for 0% Federal Income Tax, 0% Capital Gains Tax and 0% Corporate Tax; 0-0-0. Just tax consumption! Seventy percent (70%) of the American economy is based on consumption, that means a national sales tax on everything but food, gas and medicine would be a windfall. Some of America's most fiscally sound states; Texas and Tennessee for example, have adopted a sales or consumption tax instead of an income tax approach. They are running large surpluses and creating tens of thousands of jobs. Micro Entrepreneurship can close the employment gap for certain but think about how much business and investment would flow into the US if we were the most tax friendly — in fact no tax at all — nation on earth.

Trillions and trillions would pour into the country, the stock market would surge to historic heights, businesses would flock to set operations in America and tens of millions of new jobs would be created. If jobs are the underlying issue in any country, especially the major debtor nations like America, then you need to create tens of millions of them starting today. Does that sound reasonable or too simple for those representing Americans?

With our plan, every entitlement check cashed and every new dollar put in the hands of Americans is theirs to keep. If people have more they will spend more and invest more just as companies would. Therefore, the consumption tax would recoup some of the monies from entitlement checks, replace and hugely increase the revenue from the present tax system and the sales tax can be adjusted each year to balance the budget if necessary. And most importantly everyone pays and likely the rich will pay even more because they are bigger consumers. If something isn't done, the 300+ year capitalism experiment will be looked upon in the history books as just that, an experiment that didn't work.

There is a chance to turn the table. This is not a choice for us or governments, it vital to protect us from large scale social unrest, political upheaval and creating even more fertile ground for terrorist recruitment.

Hopelessness and chronic poverty are as dangerous as lack of potable water, food shortages, natural resource depletion and economic turmoil. Across the world there are tens of thousands dying each day because they can't get enough to eat and can't even drink potable water. You can live without a lot of things: you can live without food for 30 days, you can live without water for 3 days, you can live without air for 3 minutes.

But you can't live without HOPE for 3 Seconds....

The Power of Hope

John Bryant Hope, an African American leader and visionary, has been developing one of the most substantial measurements of the state of the world's population beginning with our children. Since 1992 his mission, through Operation HOPE, (www.operationhope.org), has been to bring a sense of hope to children of low-wealth communities through financial literacy education across the world.

As a result of his initial findings regarding hope and success he was able to attract the attention of Gallup that has now teamed up with Operation Hope. Gallup is using its considerable weight and research capabilities to measure how hope influences people's lives and ultimately success. The results of Gallup's recent poll showed that the most powerful predictor of academic success and graduation—more powerful than GPA or test scores—was a sense of hope. [21] Over the next ten years they will measure the effects of financial literacy and build a financial literacy index quantifying the connection between hope, well-being, engagement, and financial literacy.

This goes far beyond children, but the fact that over one billion children, one out of two in the world, live in poverty — makes this even more important. The world needs hope and now more than ever in history; the masses need hope, too. This is one of the most powerful offerings Micro Entrepreneurship delivers.

I have always said happiness is having someone to love, something to do, and something to hope for; but hope is nothing more than premature faith. Without faith in yourself you don't have a chance to do anything more or be anything more than you are today. Not only are significant organizations focusing on hope as a key indicator of success, many are beginning to expend tremendous financial and research resources to identify all the key elements which is a precursor to helping solve hopelessness.

> *"Hope Deferred makes the heart sick...*
> *But a merry heart doeth good like a medicine."*
>
> King Solomon

Hopeless but not Helpless

Let me provide an example of someone who graduated from the hopelessness of poverty into making millions that illustrates my point.

A Latino couple and their children, living in New York City ate only tuna fish for several years. They couldn't afford anything else. This couple would go through trash cans picking out discarded items so they and their children would have something to sell for money. They were like me at one time, hopeless, but not helpless. They were in poverty but they were rich in spirit. One day they found out about Micro Entrepreneurship through direct selling. They were miserable failures at first but kept trying and trying. After a few years they lifted themselves out of poverty to become millionaires. Mike and Sahi Hernandez just needed a hand up, something to provide them hope and something that changed their lives forever.

> *Change is hard to live with but impossible to live without.*
> *So do something to change for the better....*
>
> Brig

Even in America where the "American Dream" has become nothing but a dream, people have lost hope and believe the dream of once making a better life for themselves and their children is gone. Around the world, hope for a better life either has never existed or has been taken from them. Is there an answer for them and for you? The only answer to the problem is Micro Entrepreneurship. For all its names; multi-level marketing, direct selling, direct marketing and community commerce, it remains the purest form of free enterprise known to mankind.

MICRO ENTREPRENEURSHIP: THE INDUSTRY

The introduction about the world we live in is a necessary part of understanding the issues that face us all; but it is critical that we present solutions. Micro Entrepreneurship is the only solution that can have an impact large enough to make a difference. It is the only solution available to the masses that lack sufficient financial capital. It is the only solution that stands ready to be rolled out on a world-wide scale that can make an immediate impact. With that, it is then necessary to describe the industry; its size and growth and the opportunities it can afford anyone. In order to come up with a plan and present the best solution there must be a clear understanding about the Micro Entrepreneurship industry and all it has to offer.

Facebook, Amazon, Google, eBay and other Internet giants are notable for their ability to make money from you and me through the buying and selling of products, advertising or services. Almost all Internet companies have figured this out, or are hurriedly doing so. On the other hand, the industry I represent and have been involved with for over 30 years is often criticized, constrained, bad mouthed and stifled across the world. A few "bad apples" have been able to put a sour taste in many people's mouths which is what we need to address.

For over 100 years, the direct selling industry has been doing in the physical world, what online businesses accomplish on the Internet. The industry consists of a community of people buying and selling products, goods and services to each other and to those who they attract into their network to do the same. If you could buy high quality products wholesale, the same products you use every day, and distribute them for a profit while inviting others to do the same and make money from what they buy and sell, why wouldn't you? Doesn't it make sense to do that instead of going online or to a store to put money in their pockets instead of yours? Since you have to buy many things, why not at a minimum buy them from yourself and get paid to do it.

The Direct Selling industry is on the edge of an explosive expansion in a world that desperately needs it. I am helping give it a push and reaching out to every distributor and every company to join the fight. This includes you, too. This is about empowering people to take control of their lives and livelihood giving them the tools and the much needed hand up. The importance goes beyond the money. Increasing self-worth, self-esteem, pride, a sense of ownership, personal joy and empowerment to help design a future that is better than the one many have today will be transformational.

There is Only Safety in Numbers

Having the Chairman of Gallop write a book about the tragic joblessness the world faces and publically creating awareness of the issue comes as no surprise. Even former President Bill Clinton can be seen in video providing a strong endorsement about direct selling and its impact in America and around the world. Again, someone, somewhere has to do something. This not only validates the issues I am writing about, but helps propel my vision for the industry further and faster than ever before. I have tirelessly promoted this industry for decades as an answer to the many woes people and the world face. This is the most important reason I want people to read about it.

A non-profit organization, arguably one of the most influential political and socio economic leadership organizations in the world, that stays out of the limelight and hence why I won't mention their name, recognizes that hopelessness and chronic poverty are fundamental issues that among others threaten our species' future. They fully realize that if something isn't done about these issues immediately and with massive force, the dangerous world we live in will get far more dangerous. This validation is substantial. Most exciting is that they recognize that Micro Entrepreneurship can be one of the answers. I have done my best thus far to open the doors, now the industry has to come together to walk in unity through them.

I am no economist, but many smart people and organizations agree that the best way to create a massive number of new jobs today and in the future is through Micro Entrepreneurship. If the nations around the world understood the full impact of what direct selling can do for their economies and citizens they would be sure to consider loosening their regulatory grip, tax treatment and government constraints that slow and stifle the industry's growth. Micro Entrepreneurship can enable the masses, leading hundreds of millions into ownership of their own businesses and becoming economically self-reliant. Under the circumstances the world finds itself in, it is the only solution that is scalable enough for what is required.

Is there really safety in numbers? Not unless the numbers are massive. Even if the 200 biggest companies by number of employees in the world were to grow five-fold it would be only a drop in the bucket. It seems impossible to even make a dent in the numbers and thus far no way to solve it. Let me paint a picture for you and demonstrate the dilemma.

Suppose ten million new companies are formed tomorrow. Each company employs ten people. Every single one is very successful and grows to twenty jobs, doubling in size. That is one hundred percent (100%), all successful and all growing and prospering. You have employed two hundred million people. However, the next generation is being born and the children growing up today will need jobs too. Those new entrants into the jobs market need more than those two hundred million jobs, so the numbers go back far below zero.

This issue is not going away and the scenario I just painted is complete fantasy at best. If companies around the world could even create ten million jobs it would be considered a miracle. To make matters worse, the United States and various European countries, want to raise the retirement age to make up for the financial mismanagement of their social programs. People will then stay employed longer and fewer jobs will be available.

Scale and size is what the Direct Selling industry has in abundance. There are over seventy five million Micro Entrepreneurs around the world in an industry that in 2010 produced revenues in excess of $125 billion. Walmart, the world's biggest employer, has about two million within its ranks. The top fifty companies in the world by number of employees is less than the size of the number of independent business owners working for the top fifty direct selling companies. In fact, each Micro Entrepreneur in direct selling is a micro retailer, it is like having thirty mini Walmarts by number of employees throughout the world selling specialty products. A unique attribute of the industry is that in good economic times it does well, but it performs even better in down times. Not only did Micro Entrepreneurs thrive during the last recession, but the stock of the publically traded companies outperformed the market considerably.

The industry numbers are big by anyone's accounting, but still companies in this industry don't enjoy the spotlight like other companies doing essentially the same thing. I for one am out to change that.

The Industry Has Grown Up

Avon was founded in 1886 and had sales of $10.8 billion in 2010 and is part of the Fortune 500. Alticor/Amway was founded in 1959, Mary Kay was founded in 1963, Herbalife was founded in 1980 and MonaVie was founded in 2005 and was the fastest company to reach one billion in sales in the industry's history. The industry is well established, growing bigger, expanding faster and proven to create success. Success has been happening at an accelerated pace but despite approximately seventy five million people engaged, it is just scraping the surface. Compare any industry to direct selling and this industry ranks among the biggest ever. This is the power of Micro Entrepreneurship.

Going Pro

Companies throughout this industry are beginning to bring professional management in to run their businesses. This was unheard of just a short while ago. This is a very positive sign and proof that direct selling has come of age. Executives, especially those having worked at big companies outside the industry, are joining the senior management ranks. This trend has further formalized the industry's place among the most powerful industries in the world. However, people issues still remain one of the biggest impediments to further growth.

Historically, the industry has been incestuous with a company's Micro Entrepreneurs jumping from one new opportunity to the next shiny ball. Management moves from one direct selling company to another and many people try it and fail early. The dropouts get discouraged and are left with a bad taste in their mouths. They quit and never come back, yet spread unsavory views about direct selling. This taints the fertile soil for others to plant their seeds and try it for themselves. New blood in the industry across the corporate and distributor ranks has to be attracted in order for exponential growth to occur. This requires companies and the industry to do more to change people's minds, keep good people in and foster an environment where the world can see opportunity at their doorstep.

Taking the Industry to New Heights

Herbalife and Avon are prime examples of going pro. Avon brought in Andrea Jung who is the longest tenured female of a Fortune 500 company in history. She serves on the board of General Electric and most recently was appointed to the board of Apple. Avon is publically traded on the New York Stock Exchange, meaning it is really big and really successful. Herbalife was founded in 1980 and has 2.1 million distributors around the world in 81 countries. In 2011, they generated $3.5 billion in net sales which was a 26 percent increase on 21 percent volume growth compared to 2010. It sounds like the industry is growing exponentially doesn't it? It is. There are a lot more success stories just like it. [See appendix A for the top direct selling companies by sales volume published by Direct Selling News in 2011- based on 2009 sales volume]

Many of the larger companies in the industry are publically traded, a fact that many people are not aware of. Some have sales of over $10 billion a year. Alticor/Amway remains one of the world's largest privately held companies with $10.9 billion in sales in 2011. Like the Avon and Herbalife examples, they have made the going pro transition successful. But unlike the larger companies, most direct selling companies remain smaller or don't recognize the power of hiring industry outsiders to take them to the next level. Most still remain in the founders' hands and are largely family owned.

There is often very little transition within the ranks of these closely held non-publically traded companies, except in the ranks of the distributors. In these types of privately held companies senior management in the most successful and even "fallen angels" continue to remain in positions of power and in turn they continue to employ the same people. In direct selling, companies experience cycles of success and decline with only the strongest stabilizing at a certain point. Most others simply evaporate and the founders often move on to start another business, but they do the same old things with the same old people. Here is a question. How is that working out?

Often when a company is on the decline at a time when people are needed, management and many big distributors simply jump ship to the next big thing. It's the same people just wearing different hats playing for a different team. Hundreds of new direct selling companies start each year with very few successes, primarily due to the lack of power that people bring to the equation or doing the same things and employing the same ones. If you want the same results keep doing the same thing.

In Herbalife's case, they dared do things differently. They had the foresight to bring an outsider in as CEO. In 2003, Michael Johnson joined Herbalife as CEO. He had spent 17 years at Walt Disney where he was the President of Disney International before joining their team. Over a year later, the company went public, at that time sales were $1.3 billion. Herbalife is simply an example of where the industry is headed. Other companies are attracting tremendous leadership from the outside and definitely have captured the attention of Wall Street. Avon, Mary Kay, Tupperware are all household names, and now run by veterans with business experience unrelated to direct selling in their prior careers. This has been sorely needed, and thankfully the industry is recognizing it. The fact that high profile executives have joined the ranks to further build their careers is just more proof that this is a solid place to build a career for your, too.

I have direct experience with what outside influencers can do to help our industry. At MonaVie, Dallin Larsen had the foresight to bring a team in from outside the industry to help the company. He was able to hire as Chief Marketing Officer, Jeff Cohen. Cohen teamed up with MonaVie President & COO Dell Brown, now an industry leader who also came from a successful and diverse background, and the other founders Randy Larsen and Henry Marsh. Jeff came out of the media industry and had no experience in direct selling. He was part of a pioneering team that led the eBilling industry earlier and worked with multiple media companies like Turner Broadcasting and brands like Kellogg.

New management and new blood in the ranks is happening but at a slower pace than the industry needs for growth. But new and powerful forces are beginning to step in and will surely change that. Private equity investors and deal makers have now entered the game, and some in a considerable way.

Just a few years ago, the renowned venture capital company, Sequoia Capital — the people behind success stories like Apple Computers, Cisco Systems, Oracle, Electronic Arts and a myriad of others — invested $37 million dollars into Stella & Dot, a direct selling business. Warren Buffet's Berkshire Hathaway acquired Pampered Chef, and even Donald Trump entered the industry a few years ago. This is substantial, given the backgrounds and success of those companies and investors that see this industry is a place deserving attention. They put their money where their mouth is and they rarely make mistakes with their investments. That is certainly a telling sign the industry has come of age.

The industry has also attracted the best and brightest authors; business, personal development, fitness gurus and relationship experts to help train, motivate and improve the lives of millions of Micro Entrepreneurs. Paul Zane Pilzer, bestselling author and world renowned Economist, for example, has become iconic in the industry with a vision and expertise very few on this planet have. I have seen and heard him speak many times and have read his books. His insights and vision have helped this industry get to the next level. Zig Ziglar whom many are familiar with, have heard speak or read his books, has been very engaged in the industry. In 2011, he was awarded the Lifetime Achievement Award at the Direct Selling Women's Alliance (DSWA) Celebration in Dallas, TX. He even wrote the book "*Direct Selling for Dummies*". Robert Kiyosaki, author of "*Rich Dad, Poor Dad*" has brought his wisdom and personal development programs into the industry for many years changing lives wherever he goes.

Newer speakers and authors are coming into the industry every day; Keith Ferrazzi, NY Times bestselling author, Fitness Guru, Mark Macdonald founder of Venice Nutrition and best-selling author of "*Body Confidence*"; and NY Times bestselling author and Harvard professor, Shawn Achor, a renowned expert in the science of happiness, are only a few examples among dozens. Even Suze Orman had partnered with Avon as well as actress Reese Witherspoon.

Many big thinkers with big visions have helped and are helping guide the industry towards realizing its full potential.

But the potential of the industry simply can't be realized, even with all the attention and outside influencers, if the owners and executives don't come together to focus on the global issues I am describing.

Influence

The good news is that there are people and organizations doing something to change all of this. The Direct Selling Association, a powerful force that represents the industry, has become recognized around the world for its influence and strategic representation of direct selling. It has unified most of the top leaders that are working together to impact government policy, the structure of the industry and has a tireless focus on promoting this business.

In 2011, there was a flurry of Wall Street Journal inserts resembling mini magazines that Stuart Johnson, founder and CEO of Video Plus, put together that were significant. He was able to bring direct selling from Main Street to Wall Street with the support of many direct selling leadership companies. Stuart is a pioneer and has been serving the industry for decades. He publishes the industry's foremost magazine, "Direct Selling News" which further extends the industry's reach, credibility and voice. He has recently launched European and Latin American versions as well. I encourage all distributors to subscribe to this, as it contains vital information and models for success every month. It is essential that the word gets out as loudly and professionally as possible. Even with all this we are still just scratching the surface.

This industry working together can change the landscape of our world. I truly believe this. The minds, muscle and financial resources the industry has can lead the transformation of how the world sees direct selling and how the world can unleash the power of Micro Entrepreneurship the pioneers have created. Working together is the key to success and organizations like the Direct Selling Association have already taken many steps toward these ambitious goals. The next and most important step has to be taken by you. Without the U success won't work regardless of all the good work being done by others.

SOLUTIONS THAT CAN DRIVE THE INDUSTRY TO NEW HEIGHTS

The industry has an opportunity to further formalize itself among the best of breed in the world. There are limitations and impediments to growth that can be quickly overcome if all the leaders come together to do something about it. The changes are not radical but they are important, and can put direct selling on the offense.

License and Registration

The biggest reason the industry has been stifled and has gotten a bad reputation, is that anyone can get into the industry and start selling. There is little or no investment required to start your own business. That is the great thing about it and also the worst. Not everyone can play by the rules and there are bad actors that get into this business — as in any other. This is one of the reasons why there are so many constraints and so much scrutiny. The industry needs to understand that self-regulation in direct selling is not working optimally and is a missing component of success.

I believe all the direct selling companies need to come together and approach every government on earth to come up with a mandated licensing program and regulatory frameworks in partnership with them. Volunteering to work with governments to build regulations that they endorse will enable the industry and governments to realize the full potential of Micro Entrepreneurship. Successfully convincing the industry to do this more aggressively will make it prosper even more so.

For the most part, the current laws and regulations related to the industry, many created for good reason, are punitive, as compared to other industries. However, strict enforcement and oversight keeps the industry under a constant microscope. The laws exist for a reason and have been created because the majority of companies and entrepreneurs are presently self-regulated. This has required the Federal Trade Commission, for example, to play heavy-handed in dealing with direct selling. This is the same with similar government agencies around the world. In order to relax governments' postures about the industry, it is essential to work very closely with them to come up with a new model.

This is a big issue and one I have been talking about for years. In addition to the legal rules, both continuing education requirements and adhering to a high level of standards and practices to maintain your good standing should be a requirement in order to remain in the business. I believe this would help the industry to double, triple or even more in size. Amazon and eBay have good standing status for their sellers because people almost never meet the person on the other side of the screen. If a seller has a poor rating for service, is selling poor quality products or is a rip off, then their rating is low and people just will not purchase from them. It is a free market, built on trust and credibility, respect and responsibility.

Bottom line is if I cut your hair in America, and many other places around the world, sell hot dogs, sell real estate, securities, plant trees in your yard or provide almost any other service, I am required to have a license, permit or education to do so. This is as fundamental as having a driver's license or passport. In America and across the globe just being able to work requires some sort of permit. There needs to be a bar for Micro Entrepreneurs set high enough that credibility, responsibility and real accountability are firmly in place. Carrying a card that says Brig Hart, CDSP [Certified Direct Selling Professional] having met requirements to maintain the certifications will be a more powerful statement of the person and industry than another sale pitch.

Like eBay or Amazon, direct selling is a free market exercise, and many view it as having a bad seller's rating. Getting our rating back pervasively, not just within the same old distributor ranks, is mission critical to everyone's growth in the industry. Just imagine all the people that would rethink this opportunity if there was no question of its legitimacy because it was regulated and all who did business in it would have to be licensed. It is a powerful statement.

If you are already a Micro Entrepreneur, or I have convinced you to try and become one, then you have to ask yourself — are you willing to be held to standards and practices that have real ramifications. If you are thinking of selling stocks or real estate just think of their standards, the education required and the ongoing learning required. If you went through all of that work to become part of those industries would you risk not playing by the rules or just getting up and leaving it all together? Perhaps, but the barrier to exiting the business would be much harder to overcome due to the time and money you invested in yourself to become part of it.

It is obvious many companies and industries have some bad actors, but very few given the tens of thousands making a living that way. Across many industries, breaking the rules is illegal and may even result in jail time. Not to say that is the case with direct selling, but if you invest the time and money to become a professional and certified distributor, you are more likely to stick with it, play by the rules, know how to perform more effectively and be able to recruit others more successfully. If you broke the rules, personally or professionally, there would be a myriad of punitive results, not the least of which would be losing your license.

I don't think it should be a given that everyone can be in this business, although anyone can try. A hurdle has to be set and controls put in place to regulate people's behavior positively within the industry. It is essential that any new distributor who wants to participate in the opportunities direct selling can offer needs to first become licensed to do so. I have found that only 20% of the distributors produce 80% of the sales. They are pros that act like pros even though they are regulating themselves. It's the other 80% that are sometimes worrisome. I believe with the proper education, training and ongoing personal and professional development the number of top producers would double in size, at least. Sales volume and success would go way up although the total number of entrepreneurs might go down initially.

Training and education is vital. There are many industries I am not trained in. I could cut your hair and it would be a mess. I could tell you about stocks or try to stitch a wound but you would probably lose your money and bleed to death. But, I can tell you about and properly teach you about Micro Entrepreneurship. However, in order to do so I have had to build all the programs myself and actively regulate those in my organization. Although many companies have long standing and robust compliance standards internally, that alone does not do the trick. It still requires self-regulation. Compliance many times administers a hand slapping, sometimes a fine and finally, but not often, a boot out the door.

Every company needs to have certification in order for this industry to be taken seriously by others, new opportunists and especially governments. If all the leadership companies stepped up to the plate to do this, like I have pushed MonaVie to do, then any company not doing it would not be on the eBay-like best-seller list anymore. Worse, if they are unwilling to adhere to new guidelines, they would be the subject of more and more scrutiny and certainly questioned by those looking at the business opportunity and products they offer. If the big ones do it — all will follow.

Standards Body

The most successful plan that I and others would readily endorse is to have governments partner with an organization outside the industry. The business would manage the licensing and ongoing certification of all the Micro Entrepreneurs in it. I envision an independent regulatory and licensing company being established in every country that maintains the standards where everyone needs to go to pass their tests, renew their licenses and participate in ongoing continuing education. You need a license to drive in almost every country and to drive this industry further every Micro Entrepreneur should be required to have one.

Creating a standards body like the one I suggest would be a game changer for this industry. Instead of standards and good practices being an impediment to growth, as some may believe, it would be a major catalyst. More credibility would come to each and every entrepreneur and every company. This is part of the industry's Holy Grail.

Code of Conduct

A Code of Conduct is another essential element for Micro Entrepreneurs to follow if they and the companies they represent are to be successful. This relates to the issues of how distributors and companies work together and how entrepreneurs build their businesses with honor and integrity. Codes of ethics or conduct exist in most every industry and in life for a good reason. For myself, I try to walk like Jesus did, that is my primary Code of Ethics, because in the direct selling industry, some ethical standardized Code of Conduct is critical. Very few companies and entrepreneurs have a Code of Conduct that is uniformly adopted throughout their organizations and the industry has not created one like the Medical, Legal or Financial professions have. It is generally up to the individual distributors to adhere to their own Code of Conduct while at the same time adhering to the general compliance rules enforced by the company. Industry-wide Ethics and Conduct rules need to be created and strictly enforced. Like The American Bar Association, when rules are broken lawyers lose their right to practice. A similar model should be adopted by the direct selling industry.

The Distributor's 10 Commandments

For readers not yet familiar with direct selling some of the terms being used may be foreign to you. I use the word distributors because each Micro Entrepreneur buys and distributes products. Some basics terms are "up line" and "down line". If I sponsored you into my business I would be your "up line" and you would be in my "down line" and so forth all the way down with those you enlist, too. If there are problems, then my community of people must seek advice and counsel from those who sponsored them just like a chain of command in a company or in direct selling their line of sponsorship. A VP at a company or private in the military would not take a problem or issue to the general or CEO; they would talk about it with their direct supervisor first and so on up the chain. "Crossline" means that my line of sponsorship (my downline) never goes to another distributor's team or people to get counsel or advice or to have issued resolved. That is like asking someone at IBM to help or solve issues, but you work for Microsoft. The nomenclature throughout the book is fairly straightforward but there are some industry terms that need to be defined as well. Those above will help you understand some of the rules of the game and ones that I use.

The 10 Commandments are absolutes if one wants to succeed and succeed big in the industry. Most do not have the chutzpah to adhere to these and many more don't even care to implement anything like it. Those that do can attract, connect, win over and then influence others to buy into these moral and ethical principles. They will develop a solid base of followers that can then in turn replicate those values in others. These principles promote a healthy and rock solid atmosphere to grow in. They foster pure, clean air and growth.

1. Thou shall not speak Negative about the Company/Product/ Corp Leadership you are affiliated with.
2. Thou shall not pass negative information or comments downline
3. Thou shall not speak badly about or ever embarrass upline line of sponsorship
4. Thou shall not build or participate in but one distributor's Network
5. Thou shall not crossline (no sideline counseling)
6. Thou shall not borrow or lend money upline or downline
7. Thou shall not mess with another's husband or wife
8. Thou shall not do anything new for the first time without getting approval upline first
9. Thou shall honor Line of Sponsorship — No enticement ever; Zero Tolerance
10. Thou shall not teach anything in a group that can't be replicated by the masses

I have implemented this honor code for years in my business. It is my business and I want anyone associated with it to be professional and act professionally on and off the field. There is a lot of leeway given by companies, as each person owns their own businesses, but any violation of the fundamental code of conduct will not be tolerated by me and companies are starting to adopt it too.

Thankfully I have great people surrounding me and, as you will read later, that is a direct result of my positive outlook on life. It would be chaos if I didn't have my own rules even outside the corporate parent company and hopefully soon the industry will implement regulatory ones to be even more stringent.

So when you think about this industry — take all this in. This is the real deal. I'm not blowing smoke or selling widgets. I represent the company I work for with dignity and honor and I expect that you will do the same, regardless if you are new or are already in the business. You uplift the others that have welcomed you into the business and you do the same for all those you have welcomed. You speak positively about the company *always*, talking negatively is a sure way to lose and to fail not just at direct selling but in life too. These rules are simple to follow and good ones to apply in your everyday life.

Now that you have read my Ten Commandments of direct selling, do something for yourself and create and write down your own code of conduct. We should all have an honor code written and hung up somewhere, wherever you may live. It is crucial to success in this business and in life to maintain your code, but you have to write it first then have the discipline to live by it. Do it for yourself, your family and your friends. If you develop your own regulations on how you are living your life it can be transformational — believe me. Light your own candle and show others the way.

The Company – Micro Entrepreneur Bond

In the industry there are very tight and strict covenants placed on Independent Business Owners by the company. The key word is "independent." The definition of independent is free from outside control; not depending on another's authority. It means freedom in other words. Although you own your business there has to be a coupling of corporate controls and industry regulations.

As a business owner I own my business. I choose to work with a company in the industry and distribute their products. It is my hard work and effort that sells the products and it is a business that I own, not the company I am working with. For every downline distributor, it is you that brought them in. I used my own time and money to recruit them and to motivate them to sell products. Yes, I get paid handsomely and so do the distributors I brought in. But it is my responsibility to spend my time and hard-earned money to do so and my business success depends on it now and in the future. I consider all those people in my business friends and colleagues; I depend on them and what I have built, for my livelihood.

When you sign up with any company to buy and sell their products you must first read the fine print. Most every company has clauses in your initial application that once signed attach you to that company with all sorts of handcuffs and punitive recourse if you leave, join another company and especially if you solicit the people you recruited to join that other company, even though you built your own business. It sounds restrictive, and it is, but it is often the company that will come to your rescue when some of your people leave.

HOPE FOR ECONOMIC HOPELESSNESS

In fact, the rules of how you leave and the non-compete language that exists when you move from one company to another, for any reason, are there to protect you, although they seem onerous. These rules are predominately focused on independent business owners that switch teams and poach people or entice them to move to a new opportunity with them. The fact is you are building your business with the company you represent. The people you have brought into your network sign up with the company for the opportunity even though they ultimately have been recruited to work with you and your organization.

But if the company is going under, the products are not affordable anymore because of the economy or other factors and I choose not to stay with the company I cannot take what I have built with me. I understand why businesses want to protect themselves, because if the big distributors leave then it has a material adverse effect on the company and not one of us, in what we call the field, actually would ever want that to happen. But if I believe the time has come for me or you to move on or if you are new to the business and you don't like what you have gotten into, then we should be free, but with limits.

In the financial industry, as in many industries key people are required to sign non-compete agreements. They hardly ever hold up under legal challenge, but the specter of penalty remains out there and the brain damage of litigation is too much for many. People just leave and never come back, or wait a year until they can get back into it. However, even though you switch teams, and do not solicit anyone to join you, many will leave your former business voluntarily and follow you even if you beat them away.

Now in most every other industry, if a big fish was leaving or someone with significant promise was leaving there would be stock options and bonuses galore to keep them. This industry

56

does offer great cash rewards but usually not to keep you in or stop you from leaving, unless you are a top dog.

As an industry advocate, I have to address both the positive and negative challenges and issues in my efforts to bring constructive change. This area represents a sore subject, but the good thing is that many companies are beginning to lift some of these constraints. It is the company's right to protect their business. We do sign agreements when we partner with the company, but hardly ever read them again as we build our own Micro Entrepreneurial business selling their products. The flip side is if you leave and never pick up the phone to solicit one of your people, your phone will ring off the hook. Frankly, I discourage people I know from contacting anyone they had recruited for another business. I encourage you to do the same. The company does deserve our loyalty after all. However, this is one part of the industry I believe needs to be modified, though not changed completely.

I think if major distributors banded together from all the large companies, there may be a way for us to work out something more palatable with our partners, the companies. A lot of times it is the companies coming to the rescue when a big distributor in my business leaves and starts calling all my people — it kills my businesses and the company's too. The distributor rules protect everyone, but with that I think more freedom needs to be given to us to migrate our business elsewhere in a very positive way for both the entrepreneur and company.

Multi Branding

It would be a coup if, under one umbrella company, a distributor could buy and sell multiple products from multiple companies. The company pulling that off would be a huge success. But even as I write, some have figured out ways to build a niche inside of a company to do just that and represent other products not related to the business they work for to their down lines. Now that is a great solution for the issues above. It does not have to be a totally different direct selling company's products being sold, but can be other products they know their distributors want, need or would sell. It is after all my company. If I want to sell other products than why can't I? Sounds good but only a handful of distributors have been given this privilege. It would be ground breaking for a company to have multiple business opportunities and multiple products beyond the already robust portfolio of products they have. That is a big WOW factor.

Another of the likely nine ways to skin this cat is for a company, for a period of time, let us say one year, to continue to flow the residual income (more about that later) to their former partners. This would cause the distributors to change their behavior as they also have something to protect back at their former parent company. Why would they go out and recruit their own people if those people still working for the former company are making them money. The behavioral shift would really change how the industry operates and assure success for both sides.

There are many ways to make sure the parent company and its independent Micro Entrepreneurs work synergistically even in the event one leaves. I truly believe the companies that allow the greatest freedom or having multiple companies under one roof will be the big winners. Having a business that you never have to leave with the ability to move over under another of its separately branded business opportunities would be built to last for a very long time.

WHAT CAN MICRO ENTREPRENEURSHIP DO FOR YOU

Success is not a Destination it is a Journey

We have spoken about the world, the industry and will keep focusing further and further down to you and how you can be successful in this business and life. Any solution to such major issues has to begin somewhere and ultimately it comes down to you. Through you one life can be changed, or perhaps thousands, or more. The industry is about people helping people and from what you have read thus far, it appears we need everyone, everywhere to help.

Life is a journey and so is success. In most modern nations that is a well understood phrase. How many people do you know and how many people do you think actually find a path to walk on that is ever what they wanted or expected? Many have fallen by the roadside helpless, many think they can't do anything about it or become hopeless enough that they will never get up and back on their feet.

In the United States alone, this is the case for tens of millions that will never find a path out of the daily grind, government assistance or unemployment. Even if they are lucky enough to find a job out there it likely won't afford them even close to a middle class life. In Brazil, India, and China the middle class life for tens of millions is simply out of reach using typical employment models. But because of the benefits of direct selling, Community Commerce in those countries is one of the most rapidly expanding.

How can one walk with purpose and hope when there is none or never will be. For that person, their journey consists of one day after another, working long hours; one, two or three jobs just to maintain a decent life style. Their lives are consumed with making money, getting water and food anyway they can and if they are fortunate spending time with their families. In America, the breakdown of family that has turned its social fabric into burlap can be directly attributed to money, time and the lack of both. It is no different around the world.

The number one thing direct selling can provide is a chance to win back your freedom. Freedom to the walk the path you choose. Win back the freedom to spend time with your children, spouse or friends. Having the time and money to do what you want and to do it on your terms. Direct selling is not the only answer, but I believe it is big part of the equation. With freedom and opportunity I believe those countless people around the world may just have a fighting chance to be lifted out of poverty, educate their children and become productive members of modern society. That is real success.

Micro Entrepreneurship Motivates Positive Behavior

If you had told me 30 years ago that the world would look like it does now, I would have said you are crazy. If you told me unemployment, underemployment (making much less than you once did simply to have a job to buy the basics) or never having a chance to enter the work force in America, it would be unthinkable. But that is America's and the world's new reality. And many of those that have a job may be miserable; overworked and underpaid, and desperate to change their circumstances, too.

But people are not motivated by money alone. The primary motives are based on how one feels about themselves. Even those with a job have needs and wants that transcend what most people think.

Purpose

There have been countless studies done on what drives people in the world, what makes them happy and the motives for living more fulfilling lives. Although for some, money is very important, overall it is never at the top of the list. A sense of purpose is constantly one of the most highly ranked. But for those with no job or hope for a better future, the only purpose they have is another day just trying to get by or surviving. A purpose in life means being a part of something much greater than you. Something that makes you feel like you are making a difference. Rick Warren's a *Purpose Driven Life* is an example of a bestselling book that speaks entirely about this.

Billions of people on earth are simply living lives of quiet desperation. Without a way to make a living, despair and hopelessness set in and become a permanent part of their psyche. In places like Egypt and Libya, being part of something much greater meant revolution. Men and woman are simply not living out the dreams they had and many young people can't see beyond the chalk board to know there is more than just getting a job. Very few will ever feel a sense of purpose in what they do.

It is not just about the money direct selling can create for you and your family; it is that you can do something for others, too. You can be part of a greater cause by just joining the ranks of this industry. This alone is purposeful and something I want to share with everyone.

The industry is doing its part to help. Most every Community Commerce company has a significant nonprofit cause that they created that impacts thousands of people every day. One thing for sure is this industry is very giving. At MonaVie for example it is the MORE Project, where profits are contributed and distributors participate in funding its good work. At Nu Skin it is the Force for Good Foundation and Nourish the Children program. The families that own Alticor, the parent company of Amway, are some of the most charitable people in the world and Amway itself runs One by One, an award winning charity. None of the companies have to do this — they want to. There are many more like these and those companies that do give back have purpose.

Recognition

Another high ranking driver that motivates people and makes them feel more alive is recognition. Direct selling recognizes more people and does more to uplift both the most successful and those making only a few dollars a month. People want a sense of pride in what they do and validating their good work is a fundamental part of the industry's success. Companies in the industry go to great lengths to make sure any degree of success is publically lauded and all Micro Entrepreneurs do the same throughout their organizations. Success stories are recognized in print, on the Web, in video and on stages in every country where direct selling exists. This is more proof that direct selling really does value people.

Work

Interesting work, being involved in decisions and respect are people motivators that typically rank above money as well. For many that is counterintuitive. How interesting would it be to own your own business and be a Micro Entrepreneur? You are in charge of your own decisions and have the freedom to do what you want with your time again. You will earn the respect of those around you for taking the leap into owning your own business and you will have more respect for yourself too.

Money

Money is certainly a key factor. So many people on earth need only pennies, or dollars, a day to change their lives. Many are stuck in poverty with no money or the hope of ever having enough. Many are stuck in a middle class lifestyle, making money but simply wanting freedom from the daily grind. The unique thing about direct selling is you can you can start your own company with little or no investment and begin making money right away. What other business opportunity can make that claim?

Rewards

The reward for hard work really pays off in this industry. The perks and incentives given out to people for even the most modest results are extraordinary. Cars, trips, cash rewards, jewelry and so forth are just some of the rewards. Although for hundreds of millions these may not be what is necessary to motivate them, but all the same offered by the industry. A perk may be as little as a $10 bonus, and for many that can put food on the table. Regardless of what perks or incentives motivate you, the very basic idea being paid for buying things you would otherwise buy in a store, local bazaar or market place is motivating enough for most. This business "puts money in your pocket and the many perks keep money in your pocket". Giving credit where credit is due and recognizing the valuable contributions of others is at the core of this industry, so I want to thank industry veteran Jeff Graham for coming up with that phrase.

I am certain we all have different motives that drive us each day. I have only addressed a few that have been polled and researched over decades. You may not see what motivates you above, but most every motivator on the top 10 list is part of the DNA of direct selling. These factors further highlight why this industry may be for you.

YOU HAVE THE POWER TO CHANGE

The Power of Ones

Innovation, invention and aspiration can only result if one has the liberty to dream, a mind clear enough to see beyond today and a solid footing to try. I am not saying direct selling will cause a renaissance, but it will enable a lot of people to have a chance to step up to the plate. If history tells us anything, one person can change the world; Bill Gates, Steven Jobs, Henry Ford, Mahatma Gandhi, Einstein, spiritual leaders and pioneers and of course, Jesus Christ. Changing the world can happen anywhere, at any time and by anyone. But the world has not been able to provide the environment for all those people that if given a chance might change the world, too.

If this industry, governments and business leaders work together to realize Micro Entrepreneurship must be unleashed, then hundreds of millions of people will at least have a means to try and better their lives. I believe a chance is all they need. If out of those hundreds of millions, just one person is able to have the freedom to express their ideas or vision, what are the odds that he or she may also change the world? I assume a lot better than without a chance and highly likely given the amount of freed people that can contribute.

This is not just looking at direct selling through my eyes, but how millions view it and even the many others that don't even recognize it as an opportunity. You may already be in the industry or perhaps are just now learning about it. There are many misperceptions about direct selling that have been more than a challenge to overcome for many looking at the opportunity. The industry needed to be explained first before I can provide the basic tenants that can make you successful in direct selling and as a person. You are one of the "power of ones" I am writing about.

In this book you may simply find motivation from the stories of the lives of those I have been fortunate to touch and stories from others whose lives have changed dramatically because they dared to not only listen but to stand up and do something about it. The fact is, this industry only exists because of you and its success is dependent on you.

> *"Success is a decision. Has nothing to do with skill, talent or even ability...you can learn all that stuff. Success or failure is a decision you make."*
>
> Brig

There Can Be No Success without U

I am no artist or wordsmith but I can try to paint a vivid picture in your mind about me and hopefully you will see how considerable the opportunity is that this industry can afford you, too.

I was living in an 8 x 10' room on the side of my surf shop. I know the size, because I built it. All my worldly possessions included: a water bed, surfboard and wetsuit, 1000 watt per channel stereo system and a dog named Neptune. I had less than 100 dollars to my name after working my surf shop for five years, seven days a week, for 8 -18 hours a day. I was 26 years old during the recessionary period in 1978. It was not looking so good, but it is a picture of what my reality was at that time. I was busted and disgruntled to say the least. At that time, I was hopeless but not helpless. The fact was that if something didn't change for me soon, I truly wouldn't eat unless I begged or went with my hand out to someone, or worse, to the government. I was too proud to beg or take a handout from anyone. I felt so ashamed. I didn't want to be fed by someone else, or just given something. I wanted to learn how to fish.

For even when we were with you, this we commanded you,
that if any would not work, neither should he eat.
2 Thessalonians 3:10

As the story goes, I stumbled into direct selling and was taught by a historic industry leader, Dexter Yager, with the Amway business. I thus became a Micro Entrepreneur. It liberated me and freed my soul. It truly made me feel alive. Not just because I made some money, but I could really see the impact I had on people's lives including my own.

Everyone knows somebody who will.... My Story

You don't approach direct selling and think you actually know someone who will "do this thing". That assumption is usually wrong. You cannot read the minds or hearts of people. That is why I fell into the greatest wisdom of how to find folks who will take ahold and build a business.

I simply learned through innocent ignorance at first. I did with what I had and did not complain about what I didn't have. Direct selling is about people moving products and services, wholesale and retail. The more product volume you move, the more money you make. The broader and wider the structure of your business, the more profitable you will become, regardless of a specific compensation plan.

First things first. You have to find folks that want to do something, anything at first. I was recruited in February of '78 by a total stranger I met at a Jaycee meeting. I was there for the cookies and to get out of the rain. I was flat broke after working at our surf shops seven days a week, eight to eighteen hours a day for five years. Our cash outgo was greater than our income, so our upkeep was my downfall. We were spending more than we made.

We were broke, worse we were busted. I was looking to find $18 to pay a past due light bill. So the Jaycee meeting fit the bill. I had no success in getting any contributions toward my dilemma. But I met a man there who called me the next day and prospected me for his business. Why would I say no? We met and he shared the plan with me. He never asked me for any money and offered to help me get started. I did not have a clue what he shared, but I could not quit thinking about the fact that one person could help a few to help a few — all doing a small amount of business personally and replicating that through all the other people in their business. Buying some personal care and other household items from myself at wholesale, then having them delivered to my door, and getting paid for having others do the same thing was a no brainer. I rummaged through my possessions, had a yard sale to pay the enrollment fee and then got my kit and a few support tools. I was off and running.

I did everything wrong, once, twice and sometimes three times, just to make sure it was really wrong. I was hard headed and out of my league so things didn't go well for me in the beginning. I, like many, thought about how rich I was going to get fast through all my broke friends who needed this as much or more than I did.

Lesson here: People who need it do not do it. People who want more are willing to do something about it do. This is one of the greatest nuggets of wisdom I could possibly share. It took a while to figure it out, but after thirteen month process of learning how this works I went on my way to making a few small fortunes, all because of this knowledge and understanding of it. I want you to understand it also so you will be able to replicate what I have learned and what it took for me to be successful. I will tell you my story so you can possibly learn from my experience.

I got into "the business," as they called it, and made my list of all the folks I thought would take ahold and make this happen; family, friends, associates or whoever I could write down on a piece of paper. In less than two weeks I approached well over two hundred people and had little to no success in sponsoring the six I was hoping for to build my base. Not only did they say no, most were brutally honest about not wanting to be in business with me, because I had nothing to offer in their opinion. Did it hurt? You bet! It made me mad. But through this I learned that my reasons for wanting them in, was not so much to help them, but for them to help me. That did not go over well.

In the process, I was eking out a living at my surf and skate shop in Jacksonville Beach, Florida where many of the local kids hung out and lent a hand running the skate shop and park. One in particular was a little kid, thirteen years old, who seemed to shadow my every move in the shop. He loved to help out, and I assume had aspirations to be a part of the surf and skate industry someday. He faithfully did almost anything I asked of him and he became a very competent assistant for me in those days.

He outworked most of my paid employees and did it with a great attitude. Why am I telling you about him? It is because he was a perceptive young man. He saw me working my guts out to make a living but asked how I got involved in direct selling and he wanted in. I couldn't sponsor him because of his age. He just saw my enthusiasm and hope I had in it.

He watched me get turned down by everyone I loved and cared about that was of age to share it with. When the summer came Billy disappeared for a month or so. But one afternoon I got a call from him. I asked where he was and he told me he was in Atlanta, GA with his actual dad. I never knew that his parents had divorced some years earlier and he lived with his mother and stepfather at the beach. So I was quite surprised to hear he was spending the summer with his father in Atlanta. Billy was quick to tell me that his father was interested in hearing about my networking business. I asked Billy if he had shared any details with him, and said he had not.

Bill Sr. got on the phone and suggested I come up and share the details of the business with him. He said Billy was so excited about the prospect of the business that he became excited himself. I couldn't believe it. Billy gave me directions and then when I asked about what his dad did for a living he shared he was in the pipe business. I assumed a plumber or such.

This is step one…now follow what happens next. I arrived in Atlanta on a hope and a prayer and shared the opportunity with his dad. He happened to own an international construction company with contracts laying pipelines worldwide. The industry was in a recession that was his reason for looking to diversify.

His home in Georgia was exquisite. Bill and Gail were Ken and Barbie. The perfect couple welcomed me into their home so I could share how to make some money. I was intimidated to the point of sweating bullets as I shared the business and compensation plan with them. When I was done, I actually said, "and you wouldn't be interested in this I'm sure". He looked me in the eye and asked me why I would even think that. He was not only interested, he got in, bought all the support tools and products he needed to get started and hosted more than a dozen very successful home recruiting meetings. I had no real idea what I was doing, but decided to enlist the help of my up line to direct me. They couldn't believe I had sponsored this quality of partner into my business. It had nothing to do with me it had everything to do with Billy and the way I had mentored him. His father more than appreciated that action, so he gave me a chance.

From the first meeting we sponsored Bob and Alene Shreeves, a University of Georgia Professor and Engineer. They were Bill's friends and neighbors. Bob and Alene sponsored her brother and wife in Miami Florida, John and Martha Stevenson. He was a DEA agent and she was a teacher. I actually honed my skills with this group in presenting the opportunity and got pretty good at it. I traveled to Atlanta and then to Miami over the next couple of months helping John and Martha to get started.

Now picture me. I am a longed haired surfer now doing meetings in Miami, Florida with my new DEA agent friend and associates. John and Martha sponsored their first guy and gal who was also a DEA agent flying helicopters out of the Miami Dade area, Steve and Annette Woods. I did meetings for each of them as they got started. One of my first one on ones to show the plan and present the opportunity with Steve was with Bruce and Isabelle Miller.

They lived in Cocoanut Grove in a gorgeous, palatial home. He was the worldwide exclusive photographer for Rolls Royce and was Steve's fishing buddy on the side. When Bruce and Isabelle signed up I asked who they might know that would be interested in making some good money doing this. The first people they thought of was a couple that sold them their home. They introduced me to Marilynn and Bob Kuechenberg, who buy and remodel South Florida Mansions and then sell them for a profit. They thought Bob might be interested. We called and went to their home to present. Well, talk about exciting. We drove over to Star Island in one of the most exclusive areas in all of Miami. The true "Rich and Famous" hang out there. Barry Gibb was his next door neighbor.

We shared the plan and Bob jumped in with both feet. Bob was on the 1972 Miami Dolphins team that had a perfect season and he had four Super Bowl rings. Yes, Bob was now an Amway distributor in my organization. His 27,000 square ft. home was the location of the next thirty to sixty meetings I hosted. I literally moved in, and did presentations every evening for the next thirty days before Bob was to go into lockdown in training camp for his next season.

At Bob's first two meetings I presented the opportunity to most of the Miami Dolphins. We sponsored 13 players. I did not sign up Bob Griese or Don Shula, but I did present it to them. Bob and Marilynn were gracious hosts and treated me like royalty while I was with them. This part of my story all happened over a six to eight month period. I had a lot of exposure to a number of each of these people's friends, family, neighbors, and associates. We sponsored about one out of every three to five people.

Friends do what friends do and they all had credibility with their sphere of influence. I taught them to use it and not prejudge, but to prequalify. Prequalifying people is one of the most important things we did. I could have sponsored many more and so could they but prequalifying made sure we got the right people in, not just as many as we could get in. They did and it worked. But the story really only begins here.

At Bob's first meeting we sponsored a couple that were friends and were also teammates on the Dolphins, Tim and Connie Foley. Tim was a tight end for the Dolphins and quite an entrepreneur. He took to this because his sports gyms were suffering during the recession we were in. He was looking for an opportunity and this fit the bill. I worked with Tim and Connie over the next couple of months and the business just plain went wild. He was a great communicator and really caught ahold of the vision and the potential direct selling offered. The unlimited income potential hooked him. He found his niche. Now the teacher, me, became the student. Tim was a natural at contacting, inviting, showing the plan and sponsoring people. The rest is history.

Tim went through the ranks year after year advancing like only a few in the entire industry ever have. He is still is one of the most successful Micro Entrepreneurs in the world. He built and maintained a large organization that produces hundreds of millions in sales and has for the last twenty plus years. What does that mean for me? If you now understand or are already in the industry then you know it only takes a few like Tim to hit the mother lode.

When you find a few leaders in a few legs, the residual, passive income can be huge, and it was. Praise the Lord.

Now, can anyone do this? Yes. Do you know People? Age thirteen to one hundred and eight? My thirteen year old friend Billy led me to his father Bill, who led me to his neighbor Bob, who sponsored his brother in law John, who sponsored his friend and comrade Steve, who sponsored his fishing partner Bruce, who sponsored the folks who sold him his home, Bob Kuechenberg who sponsored his teammate Tim Foley. That is the beginning of a line of Sponsorship that grew into tens of thousands of active distributors around the world. Everybody knows somebody….but nobody knows who will do this, until you ask. Friends sponsor friends. If you don't have any, go and be friendly and in time you can share the opportunity too. My thirteen year old friend led me to a fortune of people that has paid me royalties for life

Although I became successful, not everyone is successful in this business. Frankly the majority of those that try it feel like failures if they are only making $50 to $100 a month. But, that can make all the difference for some. Give me $500 dollars a month and I'll take it — and I did. I started out failing at every turn. But I stuck with it and have graduated into the ranks of one of the biggest success stories in the industry.

The reality is that the majority of people trying this business give up. Sometimes it's not their fault. The biggest reason for their sense of failure is that they didn't quickly graduate in rank and earn a sizable income like the big distributors or more successful leaders that present them with the dream of cars, trips and big money. For most people, they will never get to that level and it is ok. Yes, dream big, but always remember no matter how much money you are making you are a winner.

If you want it, you have to work for it still. Just because you signed up to build your own direct selling business doesn't mean you inherited money. It is not so much the hard work, as it is working smart. Anyone can do this; it is a matter of hanging in there long enough to get the right mindset and attitude. If you think you can, you can. Some will say this can't be done, and you cannot do it….that may well be true for them, but I beg to differ. ANY ONE CAN DO IT, but many will just choose not to. I can help people do a lot of things, but I cannot make them successful. These are the only things I found out that I, or you, cannot do:

1. You can't climb a fence leaning toward you
2. You can't kiss a women leaning away from you
3. You can't nail Jell-O to a wall; and most of all
4. You can't make people successful that don't want to be.

Even though I have helped hundreds of thousands take hold of the opportunity to win their freedom, be their own boss, and do more with the little time they have on this earth there are countless more I just could not help. Like those citizens around the world in places like Greece they want a hand out, for them to be taken care of, not to take care of themselves. In the end, only you can help you. As my wife Lita says, "You have to become a participant in your own rescue if you want to make it".

I certainly didn't get a hand out, I taught myself to fish and now I have become a fisher of men and women just like you. The best place to look for a helping hand is at the end of your own arm. As the saying goes, "If it is to be, it is up to thee".

You are the Key

The Micro Entrepreneur in direct selling is the key to any company's success. This is a people-led industry and it is all about the distributors. Without a sales force, no company in any industry can survive, most of all, this one. However, as many companies grow they make the mistake of becoming "operationalized", as I call it. A big gap is created, separating and decoupling the entrepreneurs from the company. The company often forgets that the entrepreneurs are making all the money that allows them to run it, not them. Their job is to create high quality products, produce them, warehouse them, take orders, process credit cards, get the product to anyone anywhere on earth on time, provide support, pay commissions and administer the other aspects of the business non-related to selling. People move products — products don't move people.

This is not to say the business, operations and back office aren't critical, but I ask anyone out there on the corporate side of the fence to do this simple exercise.

Go home tonight. Look at your lawn, house, car and walk inside. Look at your furniture, the bills on the table and food in your refrigerator. Now call one distributor and praise and thank them for all they are doing. Because guess what? Without them you can't put gas in the car, turn the lights on, heat your house, buy clothes or eat. They are the bread winners, working hard to make you successful and for you to have a job.

The moral of the story is that it is the company's job to service the entrepreneurs. Micro Entrepreneur, independent business owner, distributor or whatever the nomenclature used, they are your client. They need service and high levels of it. At the corporate offices, there should be jumping around with joy when distributors call for help, and corporate employees should be thankful and happy to help. This relationship, unfortunately, is often strained or nonexistent as arrogance or apathy sets in on that part of the company.

Now don't get me wrong, we distributors are quite a handful. Many need a lot of care and feeding and there are thousands to service. Prima donnas exist in the industry and there are hard-to-deal-with people just like me all over. They are trying their best and expect the best in return. This is one area that sorely needs attention.

Whether companies suspect this is an issue, know it is an issue, or don't care if it is an issue — this should be an area of intense focus for all of them. Invest in your people and support them with every tool in the shed as I have done for people in my organization and the returns will be exponential. I am not saying it is everyone, and certainly not every company, but the more service the distributors get, the higher levels of respect and support received, the more products they will sell. Respect is a two-way street.

The Rat Race

I have always said that I can prophesize and tell a person all about themselves if they bring me just three things: their checkbook, their personal schedule, and a list of their personal friends. I can tell you most everything about where they are in life and where they are going. There is no hiding from the truth and the truth is 99% of people are not in the position they want to be in or never thought they would be in. Many hopes and dreams lie buried in the intellectual desert somewhere between high school and death.

American society and many around the world have trained us to be like circus animals performing on the job market stage. Go to school, get a job, get married, have kids, work your whole life and die. Not exactly that way, but you get the point. I simply can't imagine getting up every day like a gerbil running off to work, having to work for 40 to 100 hours a week for someone else in some office or a cubicle, answering to bosses, shareholders or anyone else and scraping along in the hopes that one day after 65 or so I can retire. Wake up you are 65!

What type of fun are you going to have at 65 and beyond that you should have had when you were younger, and could have had if you had been free. You cannot tell me it would not be better to have freedom when you are younger. But even if you are retired, making a little extra money to enjoy your more mature years is critical in this day and age also.

The rat race in modern countries is maintained by doling out the food that companies or the government owns. It is them feeding you and you running through a maze, not being independent and able to feed yourself. Their food is eaten readily by many and there are always seconds coming from the next promotion or social services check. In many national parks around the world there are signs that read, "Do not feed the animals. They may become dependent and not be able to fend for themselves". This is the rat race and most of the world is dependent not independent to fend for themselves. This is just like little Oliver in the movie "Oliver Twist" an orphan reaching out with a bowl just to get some more to eat or in this case a check being handed to you from someone else. There is nothing someone can do for you that you cannot do for yourself.

Even if you have a job I bet your world, your daily grind and path you are on is what I am describing. Although most of the world takes what they have for granted, they are caught up in working their lives away for someone else. Either way, there is a way to get a hand and leg up.

When I was broke and almost broken, this industry became my home and way of life. I had purpose, recognition for my hard-made money and most of all I found myself "Gainfully Self-Employed". There are tens of millions of others that just don't know that direct selling is an answer to live freer and happier and more fulfilled. With financial and personal freedom you control your own destiny and your time becomes yours again.

Why on earth would you go to Wal-Mart and buy diapers, wipes, shampoo or baby food? Why would you go get V-8 Splash Juice and other nutritional drinks when you can get the highest quality nutritional beverage on the market and make money doing it? Why buy your make up and cleaning supplies, pet food and other items like electric service, water, skin care etc. you either must buy or want to buy from a store? Are they paying you to shop there? No, you are using your precious time to go there, spending money on gas, packing the kids and or yourself in the car and then they charge you an arm and a leg for the privilege of buying stuff in their store or online. Then they mark up the price

YOU HAVE THE POWER TO CHANGE

of the products to such an extent they make billions annually doing so. That is as simple as it gets, period!

What Can You Do Right Now

First you can keep reading. I have trained countless thousands to get into business for themselves and have been personally responsible for creating more millionaires as a single individual than almost anyone, even big companies. If you are willing to do the work and follow a regiment that many distributors in the industry follow and even the company I represent, provide you with then you will inherit a plan, support structure and training to help you get started. Even though you just signed up to be a distributor you will not be left doing all the work alone. You won't be an orphan with your bowl in your hand.

New direct selling business owners can "plug into" what we call "a system" it is comprised of many things, but at its core is a body of teaching, training and motivational tools to help guide and empower both new and old business owners alike. The system will be explained further, later in the book, but essentially it provides life-long and life changing techniques not only from the most successful distributors, but the most successful and powerful thinkers that can speak to your personal life, marriage and finances, to inspire you.

Using personal growth, receiving the proper training, following a regiment of success will even make you more successful in everyday life. Helping to grow people from the inside out using these tools and techniques are essential. The key to any success in this business and any other business or job is learning, inspiration, personal growth, healing your spirit and following what others have done to be successful.

79

My previous book, "*Why Not You, Why Not Now*", can offer a kick start to anyone's career in this industry. I wrote it to tell my story in more detail and to offer a hand up to anyone who is willing to take it. You can read more about it at my Web site.

Others Will Support You

This industry hosts events like no other industry to help teach and train people to be better and do better. Gathering people is a powerful medium to use to communicate, as well as create bonds and lasting relationships, too. Every day, around the world, there are mini events in homes and hotels; there are also conventions, teaching and training seminars and national and international events. I encourage everyone getting into the business, curious or already in it to attend these functions.

Functions are very inspiring, and if you are thinking of this industry you really need to go to one. Whether it mall and large or that matter, healing your spiritout people and personal growth and tools you can use in your everyday life aris one on one, in a small group, or a coliseum of 30,000, there are people and programs already designed to help you succeed. Direct selling is about being connected and staying connected with each other to make everyone more successful. We the people are the industry and that includes you. The people support system is the most important and in this business you will never be alone unless you choose not to plug in. Others will help but it has to be you who reaches out to take and hold their hand.

Let's Go Fishing

Although I have become one of the most successful entrepreneurs in the industry's history, I continue to work at it every day.

Just because I am a spokesperson does not mean I am not 200% committed to my own success and yours.

So pick up a fishing rod or a net and I am going to start teaching you how to fish. I am not an outsider motivating and writing a book. I have lived and breathed this industry and I wish to pass along the real life experience I have had. If you are looking for a hand up, a helping hand or just the hope there is something better for you, then read on. I have shared my story with you and will present stories about what others have done and more specific "how to's". Success stories and stories of change are the best way to describe what being a Micro Entrepreneur is all about and how to create or recreate who you are. I hope you will see yourself and the opportunity before for you. This is not about me — it is about you.

First do your homework and research the products of various Direct Selling companies that you can really be excited about or that you have to buy at the store every day. I support the industry and all people in it regardless of the company they work for and the products, goods or services they sell. However, my support only goes as far as my demand that the products are superior, the founders and management of the company are great people, walk with integrity and honor and can inspire others to do the same. Management and the company have to run a tight ship and be solid to gain my endorsement and for the most part they do.

I do not support fly by night businesses trying to make the next buck or churn and burn entrepreneurs. I do not support companies whose products do not meet stringent standards and that have a clean bill of health from agencies like the FDA. I do not support companies whose management or founders do not walk with integrity and honesty or who cheat on their spouses or family. I simply will not tolerate anything but excellence in this business.

This is a partnership so make sure your partner is on par with your values and aspirations and can follow through to support your business. In order for you to make the right decision everything has to be taken in account, however, you can rely on the homework of others too if you truly trust their judgment. Even though many trusted my judgment and signed up I still encourage you to do your own homework, and a lot of it, because this step in your life and perhaps the one you have already taken needs to be taken seriously. You are not just a sales person and networker you are an entrepreneur and this is your own business.

I will present stories about MonaVie entrepreneurs, Amway and others across the industry that I have had the honor to know and many to work with. The stories of those that joined me in my most recent run are the freshest as I have been working with them for the past 5 years. Others I have known for many years or have followed their success stories. One thing to know about direct selling is that there are no secrets and words of wisdom and stories that are compelling are everywhere. I shared mine and expect to share in yours too.

I am so sure this is a place to flourish I have put my money where my mouth is. I am an investor in the industry, not just of my time but money too. My vote of confidence starts with MonaVie where just a few months ago I made another sizable cash investment into the business. I have tirelessly helped build the company and I see great promise in their mission and success. I don't want to influence your research, you have to do it for yourself and be very careful about it. Being diligent up front before you jump in will make a big difference in your success. Knowing the ins and outs of the business and the business opportunity will help you spend your time wisely. Always keep in mind that time is truly the only currency we really have in the end.

I Am All In

My latest run started in 2005. My research lasted for over a year
before I even considered jumping back into the industry. I stayed
out of direct selling for years after Amway and took a lot of time
to consider getting back in. Once I am in — I am all in and for
me that means a 24-7 worldwide commitment. So I have to
careful of what I get involved with as I choose to invest all of my
discretionary time in the very thing that rewards me the most
for that time spent. I know most everyone reading this cannot be
"all in" but even a toe in the water can make a real difference in
your life. Whatever time you choose to invest, do it with all your
might….don't do it half way. People will follow those that are
passionate, convicted and excited.

It started when I began hearing a lot about this berry called
Acai and its health benefits. I began drinking a juice derived from
the Acai berry long before acai was vogue. I could really feel the
benefits in the first few weeks. It was something that actually
worked for me. I had really drunk the Kool-Aid.

So I set out to find out where this great product was coming
from. My research led me to Dallin Larsen then the CEO of
Monarch Health Sciences and now CEO of MonaVie. I imme-
diately knew this was a man that is going to do something great.
This is not unlike others like Blake Roney, one of the founders of
Nu Skin, the Devos and Van Andel families that started Amway,
Mary Kay or the now deceased founder of Herbalife Mark
Hughes. They were all visionaries and industry pioneers.

And that is how the story goes. I took my time. I was very
thoughtful about the products, did research on Acai, the
company and the team. When you have great products and great
people there is a winning combination. So do not jump at every
opportunity especially if you choose to make a career out of this

industry. But if you do commit to designing your own future then get all in like me and I am certain you will get results.

However great the juice and weight management products I represent are, the price of the products or the business opportunity may not be something you can get behind. It may just not be the right product for you or be able to enlist your passion. For many, another business opportunity and quality products may be more in line with what you want to do. I know for all those whose circumstance include poverty or living day in and day out just making it many businesses and opportunities offered will not support them and the community of people around them that are likely in the same position. Those people may need much cheaper products that can be afforded in some cases for pennies a day in order to be successful. This industry has opportunities for them too.

My network of leaders, Micro Entrepreneurs and I were able to empower over a million people to drink the product not just because of its great nutritional benefits but many of them saw the opportunity to earn money as well. It was fulfilling to see people and to hear their stories about benefiting from the product but even greater was enabling them to make money buying it and brining more and more people along to try it and sell it too. It wasn't easy at all but it was rather simple. The company delivered on its promise and we delivered over $1 billion in sales in less than three years.

Prior, I created my own direct marketing insurance business and before that I was at Amway a company many people already know. I was recruited into the Yager line of sponsorship, and was fully mentored by his Teaching and Training System. He, like Bill Britt, another big Amway success story, built entire companies to provide tools, training and motivational content. Those tools and training kept me connected and helped me grow as a person so I could flourish. I made sure everyone I recruited also used a systematic way to build their business and to stay connected with me and the organization. Without that connection so I could stay focused 24-7 I would have failed. The importance of staying connected to others that have offered you this opportunity is vital. You cannot just go home after a meeting and having signed up to build a business without mentorship either digitally or directly.

Over the years with the Amway business, my personal and group sales totaled well in excess of $5 billion in sales over a 12 year period. While helping hundreds of thousands of people and their families I, even more importantly, was given the opportunity to speak wisdom, spiritual healing and hope into their lives. Hope and believing in yourself are critical in everyday life and breathing that into people is my greatest calling and mission. For me the primary goal has been to inspire and change lives not just to make another dollar. This mission through direct selling has become a reality and it takes all the faith and energy that I can muster.

74% of the population in America has purchased products through the direct selling industry at some time. [22] Industry leaders and companies are everywhere and so many people benefit from selling Nu Skin, Vowerk & Co., Stella & Dot, Primerica, Amway, Natura Cosmeticos, Mary Kay, Avon, Tupperware, Herbalife, and other house hold names all over the world. In my case, MonaVie has benefited me and my family and associates greatly, just as Amway did in the first chapter of my networking career.

When you do your research make sure to look through all the trash talking on the Internet about the industry and companies. Unfortunately, with the Internet anyone can say anything about a company or about people and almost all of it is simply untrue but unsettling for many all the same. This is the primary deterrence from taking a chance that this can change their life. Get past that and you will find that these companies, and that doesn't include all of them, are credible and are run by serious and many inspiring people.

I am sure this all sounds great and rosy but you have to want it. The industry can lead you toward a better life but it is you that has to take responsibility to do it. I encourage you with as much passion as I can to get into this business. I especially believe for stay at home moms and even those that can make a few extra bucks this can make all the difference in your life.

ONE STEP AT A TIME

If you are reading this then you have already begun to understand what Micro Entrepreneurship can do and how necessary it is for the world. But in order to do something about it you start with putting one foot in front of the other and understanding the basics of how to do it successfully. If you are already a Micro Entrepreneur then pass this book along to everyone in your downline, those at other companies and those interested in the opportunity. They will benefit from the wide variety of topics contained within and also learn the ins and outs that you may already understand.

Walk First

1. Do research and find a product or suite of products that you either buy every day, such as necessities for your children or products that make you look good, feel good and you buy from stores anyway. Don't line the store's pockets, line yours. I repeat this often because it is the most import factor in your success and the most basic way to understand that what you may buy every day can benefit you financially.

2. It is critical that if you know anyone in the industry then seek them out. Ask questions but don't be pressured into the opportunity. Talk it over with your spouse, friends and family to make sure you have a support structure on the home front. Even if you have tried this before for whatever company I encourage you to come back and just give it another chance. It really does work especially if you follow a success system like those I have created and participated in creating.

Pick up the Pace

3. Attend an information meeting if you can determine where one is. Inquire online and find one in your local area and most of all find an existing distributor to help you learn more about the business and the products you have chosen to pursue. Let them educate you about the industry and products and people. You will find amazing people that will surround you and help. This industry isn't about the companies it is about the people. Without you and me the companies can't exist. Let those who know guide you.

4. Just do it. Sign up. Buy the product. Buy some business and teaching tools and things that can help you plug into the network and others that can improve and inspire you as well. Most of all follow what successful people are telling you. This takes discipline even it is part time to succeed. If you follow the guidelines that have been vetted for over 30 years you will have success even if it is a few extra dollars a month. We can all use what we can get especially in these dire economic times.

Gidee Up!

5. Spread the word. I asked people early in my career; do you use toilet paper. Of course you do. Would you purchase it from yourself from now on and get paid to do so. Well that is a no brainer right? It really is. That alone is a big deal. Believe me the people you talk to will get it so talk to everyone you can.

6. Identify your community and do not be shy or embarrassed to ask. Make a list. Write down as many people as you know and then call them. My first distributor was my mother — how is that for up close and personal. I thought I would have to build a whole network around her but she went out and recruited

dozens that turned in hundreds that turned into thousands. You are introducing them to an over 100 year way of buying and selling. It is not a scam as you will read across the Internet and about virtually every company in the industry. It is real and can change lives. Have fun and make money but most of all win your freedom to live a more prosperous life. See if that doesn't get their attention.

7. When you have the opportunity to introduce the industry and the direct selling opportunity be prepared for many no answers or Yuk! That is a terrible industry. In many circles it is simply a dirty word. This barrier exists because of misperceptions and trash talking that is mostly untrue and the black eye that I am working hard to remove from the industry. It is Community Commerce, just like buying online except it is offline. This is a phrase my partners and I introduced and I expect it will have a material impact on the way people view the industry. Even the company I represent has adopted it as the new terminology that accurately represents this business. Call it direct selling, multi-level marketing or direct marketing — I call it Micro Entrepreneurship. This is very important because it will help overcome the biggest objective you will get — the reputation of the industry.

8. Adapt and overcome and most of all be proud of what you are doing. Google does what direct selling does as do Amazon, eBay and others. Those names get people's attention in the first minute of the conversation and it dapt and overcome and especially be pround. Google does it, Amazon, eBay and others. That gets attention but its true. m youis true. They sell you stuff don't they. They incentivize you to sell ads and get your friends to sell ads. They pay bounties to drive people to their Web sites to buy products and services. Doesn't that

sound like Direct Selling? They ask you to join their community and for others to do the same. Ultimately, they want you to buy things.

    a. Here is an example of how to introduce the industry and yourself as Micro Entrepreneur. Ask someone. "Have you heard of eBay, Google, Facebook, Amazon?" Of course they have. "Have you heard of Avon, Nu Skin, Tupperware, Mary Kay, Herbalife, MonaVie, Amway and so forth?" Most likely yes. "What if I told you they do business the same way, one online and one offline?" They will probably look at you strangely. "Well they are! I am a Micro Entrepreneur and I found that any community of people buying and selling things to each other and making money from those doing the same is what direct selling does just like many the big Internet giants. It "vite others to do the same that i Internet giants." things to each other and making money from those doing the same is what diis simple. I buy products for myself that I need or want and I invite others to do the same. I make money doing it for me and money from all those doing it for themselves. It is like selling ads on the Internet or getting paid to promote a product and helping Internet sites get more traffic. It is a real business that Donald Trump built a company around a few years ago. Warren Buffet's company acquired Pampered Chef, a direct selling company a while back, and even the famous investors behind Apple, Cisco, Oracle and Electronic Arts invested in a direct selling company just 2 years ago. Even better I don't go to my local stores to buy as much stuff as I did before. Why would I go through the hassle of standing in lines, driving to the store, especially with gas prices they way they are, and they don't pay me and either do Amazon or Wal-Mart. Do they pay you to buy things from them?" NO!

9. Finally, stick with it. Success and even those extra dollars may not happen overnight. You may get discouraged right out of the gate and many people may say no regardless of how hard you try. Don't quit! Keep stepping up to the plate and you will get results perhaps right away but I am certain eventually. Keep trying even if it is way outside your comfort zone. If you find some discomfort in the sales part of doing this business or just do not feel that you can do it then you can use the products and services I have invented that provide you with a personal selling team to take the burden off your shoulders. You can simply introduce the idea and let someone else do the selling and bring them along into the opportunity. You can learn more about the product and services at my Web site. There are countless ways to succeed and failure rests on your ability to just have the guts and the drive to do it.

If you get past the first no in a few minutes then you have opened the door to present the products and business opportunity. This is where the tools and training that experts have taught you or that you have picked up out of this book become critical. Once you can get someone focused on the bigger idea of personal freedom, financial success and great products you have to be able to put your training to work.

Always remember your ABC's. Always Be Closing. Always be filling your pipeline of prospects and suspects. The more you speak to others the more of them that may follow. However, just brining someone into your business doesn't mean success for you or them. Many in the industry forget this is about quality not just quantity. If you have quality people that really want it — and you will know it when you speak to them — you will flourish as I have.

If you want to see more then go to (www.brighart.com) and dig in. I want to help you help yourself. As I said it is more important for me to speak into your life for financial, spiritual and personal freedom and fulfillment than making just more money. The water is warm. The industry is hot.

BASIC TRAINING

How You Make Money

Compensation in direct selling, or Community Commerce as we call it, is achieved in many ways. Each company develops a plan that when you begin selling their products and inviting others successfully to do the same your revenues multiply. It feeds off itself and often takes on a life of its own.

One of the terms I will use to describe a Micro Entrepreneur's business is legs. Yes you will use your two legs, but legs in this context means the people you recruit directly beneath you. If I recruited two people, I would set each one up under me and I would have two legs. I then help my partners build and build as much as I can beneath their legs to make them more successful. You can have any number of legs but the real cash flow comes from moving product. I will describe a few plans below and you can see in Appendix A some of the plans used in different companies.

In the direct selling industry, compensation is one of the reasons folks get in and stay in a particular network. There are many variations of compensation plans offered by companies but most fall into two types; Binary and Unilevel Compensation plans. Both types of plans pay out a certain percentage of the overall gross sales volume to the distributors that are creating the sales volume. Legitimate companies and compensation plans do not pay for sponsoring people, they pay for the sales volume created by that distributor and his or her organization.

People get into Community Commerce for many reasons, but in the end it is the money. I got in for the goodies, stayed in because of the people, and built it big because of a cause. I fell in love the fact that I could actually help influence people's lives for the better. It became addicting. But hear me clearly, if you don't make the money, the people will not stay and build, because they cannot afford to. In the end, "it is a business".

Binary Compensation Plan

The premise of the Binary Compensation Plan is to pay out to the entrepreneurs who structure all their contacts and enrollees in two legs. Both personally sponsored and those built deeply beneath them are placed in either a left of right leg. The key is to maximize the sales volume in each leg and the companies pay on matched volume. Sounds as though you only need two folks sponsored, but that is a myth. Why? Because rarely do the two folks you sponsor do anything. You will in most cases have to sponsor 10 to get one to perform and continue to do the activities that create the volume needed to produce profit.

It is normally, as I shared earlier, not those you have personally sponsored but the people they sponsor and those that they sponsor in depth that creates a fire so to speak. It is the collective effort of that line of sponsorship that creates an atmosphere that continues to attract more folks. Success breeds success in this area. Most folks want to be a part of something that is happening.

As the leaders are found, or developed, they keep the rank and file folks engaged and producing. With a good system that can offer the information and knowledge they need, along with the motivation and inspiration, people tend to stay engaged long enough to see the results they are working for. There is no magic in creating volume, it all comes from sponsoring folks who buy the products and move them on a consistent basis.

Unilevel Compensation Plan

The Unilevel Compensation Plan pays out on the number of legs you personally recruit and those that produce. These are the people I described and for ease let's call them the first tier of your business. The wider or more people you personally sponsor the more profitable you can become. Simply put, the more legs you have producing volume the more companies will pay you. It is really as the saying goes "more feet on the street".

Whatever the percentage is in any compensation plan, the person who sponsors the most legs that produce the most volume will make the most money. You cannot pay folks on just their numbers. Each entrepreneur in the organization that produces volume consistently, week to week or month to month, will get paid consistent commissions. The model is straightforward and most companies set up Autoship for products being purchased. This means when you start buying products they are shipped to you each month and the longer you and others stay on Autoship the more money you make. The basic premise is the wider and deeper those legs grow, the more profitable you become.

Hybrid Compensation Plan

The newer companies in the industry have adopted a hybrid of both compensation plans. A Binary married to a Unilevel. There are three to ten ways of making money or commissions. Some are; retails sales, sponsoring bonus for those getting on Autoship, commissions on cycles in the binary, bulk order bonuses, leadership bonuses for developing volume in your group, overall commissions for the volume your group produces from the legs built all the way down from the top tier and up to level ten, which is a lot. There are also level bonuses for hitting higher volume levels that have a pin, or rank, associated with it. For example you can advance to gold, ruby, emerald, diamond and so forth and get bonuses and increased compensation pay out at each new level. Helping others achieve a new rank also pays a bonus, so you are rewarded for what direct selling is all about; people helping people. Maintaining certain sales volumes over the weeks or months throughout the year can pay bonuses also, like profit sharing or founders bonuses. It does not matter what they call them, most companies pay out 20% or more of their profits to the entrepreneurs in just bonuses and perks. Ultimately, the companies can pay upwards of 50% to 60% of profits to the entrepreneurs in their compensation plans.

All companies claim to have the best products and compensation plans. A simple audit can help determine where they actually stand. What percentage of their gross volume is paid out in bonuses and perks will inform you where they are positioned in that business category.

It all comes down to who can recruit the most folks that consistently move the most products and services. If I produce a lot of sales volume for a short time period it does not produce ongoing income. Hundreds and thousands doing a little bit, every week, or month produces ongoing income. This is especially advantageous when the products being purchased are used personally, used up and bought again by the masses. These are the products people need to buy or otherwise like to buy, for example make up or vitamins. Those types of products are expended and replenished each week or month so reorders and ongoing Autoship continues.

Direct selling 101

Success begins with you, your belief in yourself and your desire to do something about your circumstances. I weed through people very quickly and realize that many just won't do what it takes. People don't make it in networking because they are either:

Ignorant. They do not fully understand the business they are getting into, they listen to others that have failed or believe what they read. They do not follow the formulas for success handed down and taught over decades and most of all they simply don't care to and think they can do this business just their way.

Lazy. You can lead a horse to water but you can't make them drink but you can salt their oats and see how fast they drink the water. In other words, if someone is hungry enough, desperate enough to change their circumstances or simply looking for a better tomorrow then they can have it but not by sitting around.

Doubtful. They do not believe in the opportunity and hesitate to pursue it with vigor. Worse, they doubt themselves and are already set up for failure. Finally, they doubt they can ever change so they just bury their head in the sand.

Many will try this business and not see results right away and then just give up. It takes guts to change your life. It takes discipline and proven processes to give you a fighting chance.

I have achieved success in almost of all of things I have supported. But at the core I am just like you. I wasn't handed anything except for a hand up. That one hand extended to me changed my life. This book isn't just about the state of affairs of the world or the industry it is about your state of affairs and many like you.

Being a Micro Entrepreneur in this industry is not selling snake oil and I am not PT Barnum. I am Brig Hart and I wake up every day looking at him in the mirror and asking 2 questions; God can you help me grow and prosper today and what am I going to do to make that happen. I ask myself those 2 questions because we all need help to do the things we are called on to do.

I assure you that you need every bit of help you can get in business and in life to be successful. Those two questions no matter what you believe in spiritually or perhaps different questions can dramatically change the outcome of the today and day after day doing so creates a successful path.

Direct Selling 102

No matter what you believe in first you have to believe in yourself. This whole industry and this opportunity or anything else you may do will not be successful if you don't believe. This book or my words may never change your beliefs and I know that when I meet people. That is why I look for those who want to learn how: how to be a better person, how to lift and free one's spirit, how to walk a faithful and honorable path and most of all get a rod in hand and go fishing. If you have your hand out and expect to change your life by living off of someone else's or government assistance forget it. You are not in control of your destiny — they are.

Strong or Weak

One of the keys to success in anything you may do is to know your strengths and weaknesses. I don't cut my lawn anymore. Why? Because there is someone better at doing that than me and my time is more valuable when spent doing other things that I am good at. My beloved wife Lita, who has been by my side, for richer or poorer, manages the finances. Why? I assure you that she is much better at it than me. I know my strengths and one is reaching out to people to help them help themselves. And that happens to be direct selling 101 and why I have had success in it. But I cannot help you and you cannot help you if you don't know your strengths or weaknesses, get motivated and wake up and stare in that mirror. And that is life 101. It starts with you and ends with you!

Now the fun starts. You want to make money and have fun. Sure everyone does and Gina Merritt says that better than anyone. Steve and Gina Merritt are a few of the most successful industry distributors. They started small and followed the formula I spent 30 years developing. In fact, they followed it to a tee. However, if it wasn't for them waking up every morning asking themselves "what can I do today to be more successful and to do better than I did yesterday?" they wouldn't be multi-millionaires, and neither will you if you don't do the same. Steve and Gina's book will be coming out shortly and is a must read for anyone looking for inspiration and to build belief in themselves.

It does not matter how slowly you go,
so long as you do not stop.

Confucius

Start small. The heart of Micro Entrepreneurship is: Buy from yourself, merchandise a little bit, and tell others to do the same. Or simply put: Use — Merchandise & Teach.

I was demoralized when I was younger although I did believe in myself. You may be so stuck in your rut or never have the chance even offered to you to look in that mirror and call a spade a spade. You believe soap or a laundry detergent like Tide will clean your clothes don't you? You believe vitamins, fish oil or other nutritional products will help you be more healthy don't you? But what about you! Do you believe you can do more than you are doing? Are you lazy or a procrastinator? Are you good parent, friend or employee? Don't lie! This is real chance for you to evaluate yourself and find what you are good at and not good at. Here are my strengths and weaknesses:

Strengths
I trust God more than myself
I know my limitations
I will show up when I say I will be there
I am quick to acknowledge what I don't know
My Wife
My kids
My friends
I am not afraid to ask for help
I always do the best I can with what I have
I have a very optimistic outlook on life
I love most folks and like few
I have a keen sense of what is real and not
I love to give
I am addicted to seeing people succeed
I appreciate my placement in life...born in USA
I had a great legacy left to me by my Parents
I have a strong sense of direction
I believe in people beyond what they believe in themselves
I know my gifts and talents
I can always see ways to improve just about anybody and anything
I am not afraid to tell the truth
I love my life...daily

Weaknesses:
I believe in people's goodness beyond what they many times deserve

I am too proud to ask for help at times
I'm a horrible manager
I am too self-involved and consumed with my interest vs.
others
I tend to over assist folks in overcoming
I don't listen to my wife enough
I am a great mentor to others, and not as good to and for my
kids
I like hot rods — fast cars and planes
I am impatient with myself and others

You see I am brutally honest. To start a successful career, any career, especially direct selling you have to know who you are and what you are good at. Accept those things you are not good at and improve the ones that can most help and leverage your strengths. You may be great with numbers, you may be a great fireman, policeman, farmer, doctor, lawyer, mother, maid, financier, student or simply a good provider even if it is just bread and water or a clay home or shanty hut. You may live in a tent or your car. You may be unemployed or flipping burgers. You may be struggling with a death, divorce and worst of all hopeless that things will never change and this is the way it is and always will be. Build on your strengths and staff your weaknesses.

No matter what your circumstances you can take out a pen and paper right now.

Stop!

Do not read another word and just do yourself a favor and write them down. Really think about it and don't just throw anything on the page. You can also go online and take a free personal assessment or one you pay for but they are all pretty cheap. I encourage everyone do this. Ask people around you what they think. That is always very telling and usually the most accurate.

What did you write down? Good at your job? That is not what I am talking about. Are you a good student or Fireman or Doctor? Not what I am talking about either. Those are things we do, not who we are. But your strengths and weaknesses will contribute greatly to what you do for certain. This exercise is about you. Direct selling 102 starts with you and if you don't know yourself or don't want to then stop reading and go right back to what you were doing. But before you do ask yourself this important question — how is that working for you!

If you wrote down I am smart, I am a good person, I am good with people, I do not lie or cheat, I can run fast, good at sports, a good speaker, healthy, can read people well, can inspire, can win a jury, can open a chest and operate on a heart, can pick stocks then these are all things about you. Now on weaknesses if you say I lie, cheat, I am unfaithful, I have no hope, I don't have confidence, I follow others, I judge people, I look bad, I am fat and ugly, ignorant, lazy, doubtful or any number of others then you are honest. We all have faults but unless you are really truthful you will never look in the mirror and wake up asking yourself; what can I do today to be more than I was yesterday. How can you? You don't even know where you are starting from. To change anything about yourself or a business or your family or your circumstances you first have to start with knowing yourself and believing you can change.

Knowing yourself is the beginning of all wisdom.

Aristotle

Direct Selling 103

Picture what success is to you. If I only could make an extra $100 a month I can save and go on a vacation. If I make an extra $200 a month I can buy new clothes for me and my family. If I made an extra $300 a month I could afford better healthcare or pay for my medicine. If I made an extra $500 a month I could send my son or daughter to a private school or buy a new car. If I could make ten cents today I can eat for a week. If I made one dollar today I could even save my life. Whatever the need is direct selling can be the answer. Even if you only have two people, three people or thousands of people as part of your business you will still make some money. Even with one or two people in your business you may be able to get some or all of your products for free from the money you earn. But the best thing is as long as the people you have in your business keep buying the products and hopefully getting more people to buy them you get paid. That is magic. RESIDUAL INCOME! In other words it keeps on coming even when you are sleeping. Now doesn't that sound good?

So what is success to you? Is it a better life for you and your kids? Is it to eat for a week? Move out of a slum or most of all to be in complete charge of your life or destiny. You want to flip burgers for the rest of your life? I doubt it. You want to clean someone else's house for the rest of your life, or lay brick, or give out speeding tickets. I doubt that too. Whatever the career, whatever the path you are on it can change.

Walking the Walk

I have found the most important things to me are faith and family. There is no greater investment you can make than in your faith, whatever that may be, and there is no greater success than investing in your children, marriage or friends. So ask yourself is it worth it to make some extra money to help your children grow and prosper. I bet you answered yes.

Holly Roush asked herself that very question. She was a business executive that decided to stay at home to be closer to and spend more time with her children because she loved them. But she wanted to do something even better for them than she already was. So she did something about it! She found direct selling and was hooked. She didn't have a bunch of friends and family to go to but she started there. She believed that if she introduced products and the industry opportunity to others they would be inspired to do what she was doing.

Her husband Corbin wasn't a believer. In fact he shunned the whole notion of direct selling. He shared the same misperception that many have about the business. Success breeds success and she was successful at changing his mind for sure. They just bought a new house, live free to do whatever they want with their kids, whenever they want and by the way became multi-millionaires. Her story is a great example and her latest book "*Holly Would*" documents her path to success.

Collette Larsen is a USANA distributor and has been for a long time. She rose through the ranks to be one of their top producers. Her story of making money is not unique but her life story is very inspiring. Many women become very successful in this business and she is one of them. But it is not all about money. She has a child with a life threatening illness and recently her daughter had a very successful surgery, one that was very expensive and had to be done. What if she hadn't been successful? What if she wasn't free to be with her family day and night not just through this circumstance but over the years? What if she didn't have that extra money and the resources to make sure her daughter was safe? Think about it and what you are doing today to make sure you are successful at what you do and if you could be successful at direct selling and earn those extra few dollars, hundreds or thousands or millions what that would do for you and your family.

There are tens of thousands of these stories I have collected over the years. You will only read about a few in this book. I have shaped many success stories and worked with people that have dramatically changed their lives, those of others and especially my own. They held up their dream and made it reality.

My experience at MonaVie and Amway include success stories from doctors and lawyers, single moms and stay at home parents, firemen, policemen, teachers and the poverty stricken. Randy Schroeder, Bob Robinson, Randy Haugen, Mark McCormick, Todd and Angelique Hartog, Jan Prpich, Charlie Kalb, Ken Porter, Orrin Woodward, Frank Soucinek, Shelly Aristizabal, Mike and Sahi Hernandez, Al and Sherry Huva, Onyx Cole and so many more overseas like Shah Khan, Johnny Chia and Akira Tamai in Japan, all with very diverse backgrounds and prior careers, have become big successes in the industry. There are countless others like Dexter Yager and Bill Britt at Amway, Steve and Melyn Campbell, Barry Chi & Holly Chen at Amway, Enrique & Graciela Varela at Herbalife and thousands of Micro Entrepreneurs around the world at Ignite, Unicity, USANA and Shaklee have all had similar experiences. The top distributors in this industry have become very successful and their businesses keep producing residual income. [See Appendix B for the industry's top earners in 2010]

I can name thousands that I have been inspired by and have inspired, but this book would be nothing but the long list of them. So I will apologize to all of you that know me from many companies and even those that are very close to me that I couldn't mention.

The fact is these are people that stood up and took the step into direct selling and I trust that you can do the same even if you are already a part of it. You may not become one of the top earners but if I could inspire all the stay at home moms alone to be a part of this industry then their children, family and they would make the biggest difference and not just in America but around the world. Take a page out of John Hope Bryant's work on the hope index. Sometimes hope is all you need to start — hope and belief — and those 2 things can change anyone's life, anytime and anywhere in the world.

Direct Selling 104

A support system is essential in direct selling as it is with anything in life you do. Many of us have some support systems in place already. Family, friends, colleagues, books, television or whatever helps them make it through the day and have hope for tomorrow. But many more don't have families, friends and circumstances that have left them all alone in the world. They join gangs, wallow in self-pity, spend day in and out in their 4 walls or in factories and the fields living alone. But no one wants to be alone. They are truly stuck and one reason this industry, more than any other, is for them. This industry is a family made up of supporters, advisors, mentors and people that will just outright care about you.

Systems exist in direct selling to help you build and grow a business but more critical is the ongoing personal growth in all areas of your life that is provided. Many companies fail to provide their business owners with the tools and training necessary to succeed, so many distributors just walk away. Why? It wasn't

because they didn't try it as millions of former industry partici-
pants did. It was largely because they were left to fend only for
themselves. Granted they have to be an active and willing participant, but for 30 years I have accumulated knowledge and wisdom
that is shared with people wanting to be a part of the industry.
Leaders in the industry try hard to encourage, coach, enrich and
touch the lives of thousands. It is impossible to stay connected
to everyone every day and this is why a systematic way of doing
business in this industry is essential. Plug in and get connected.
You will become a better person, have quality people in your
life and not be left alone. Most of all it will greatly enhance your
chances of success.

The Basic System of Success

Books, CDs, videos, online training, events, spiritual guidance and
healing, and education are the basic things that make up a system.
You see it is comprehensive and focused on helping you build
your business and a better life across the board. Who doesn't need
some of that? The tools and learning manuals offered are essential
to making sure each individual that has chosen to be a part of an
organization can feel connected, and stays inspired enough each
day just to make that next call or have another face to face meeting.
However, the business tools represent only a small fraction of the
system, it is largely about personal growth. Growing people grows
business and as the business grows so does success for you and the
companies you represent.

The top performers that I know in this business promote this
vital component vigorously. The systematic way to build your
business and to follow the success of others is so important that
MonaVie worked with me and many other distributors to create
MVP, the first corporate system being used to create uniformity

and keep everyone connected no matter where in the world they were. The MVP system is something I am proud to have helped because it does more than just teach the business, it teaches a person how to be better; a better family member, better financial steward, better mom, dad, husband, wife and most of all a better person.

Self-help, inspirational and business books, teaching and training has become an industry producing tens of billions of dollars a year. McDonald's, Starbucks, IBM, Microsoft and most every company you know have robust learning systems and standards and practices that they employ uniformly everywhere in the world. The Chief Learning Officer has emerged in most every major organization as a vital component for growth and retention. This demonstrates that the power of a systematic way of doing business and a code of conduct, learning and training breeds success.

Having a system is even more necessary in direct selling. Call it the brain of the industry and given the fragmented; spread around the world, Micro Entrepreneurial nature of direct selling every single company should have one. A successful system is comprised of Seven Pillars.

Teaching is the primary tool used in this industry to help others replicate what the most successful entrepreneurs have done. It is the "what to dos" and the "how to dos" of building yourself, your business, your finances and your relationships. Teaching plants seeds and lays the groundwork for people to be trained. Many people confuse or lump teaching and training together.

1. Training is unique in our industry because we are in the people business. People need to be trained by showing them how to do something. You can teach someone that a round

peg goes in a round hole, but the training comes in when show them how the round peg physically goes into a round hole. Training = Showing.

2. Motivation is an outside influence. People need encouragement in the form of positive CDs, DVDs, speakers, books and so forth. They need their senses to be motivated each day because we are constantly barraged with negative influences. If you believe, you are motivated. Teaching motivates, relationships motivate, situations motivate, music motivates. Stay excited!

3. Promotional Items. In direct selling you are building a brand around products, the systems, the company and most of all yourself. Promotional items are meant to build awareness like stickers on your car, hats, tee shirts and I go as far as suggesting people turn their cars into walking billboards. Do it first class. Do it with quality. You need to shoot for excellence, not perfection, but you want the people you are working with to look good and feel good. You have to take ownership and brand yourself 24/7 — it is after all your business.

4. Clear communication in this industry is the key to staying connected and keeping momentum. We live in a real time society and there is more than enough information to process. Good, reliable communication and information permits progress. While nothing takes the place of eye to eye, there are so many other ways to stay connected — websites, phone systems like Vie-Comm (electronic voice mailing), phone, e-mails, web conferencing, VT (Virtual Training). Communicate effectively and often and it will nurture those you have introduced into the industry to stay with it longer and be more successful.

5. While motivation is external, inspiration is internal. Inspire means "in the spirit." It is long-term and can help someone to understand his or her true makeup. For me inspiration comes by the word of God such as through New Life Network, the MORE Project and inspirational books, CDs and sermons. You may find inspiration in other forms or beliefs but it remains central to the health and wellbeing of others you are working with.

6. Helping people to plan their work so they can work their plan is critical. The calendar of functions and events is crucial to gather your business partners where you can speak to them all frequently. Companies and business owners organize everything from the smallest events to the major functions. Open meetings, nuts and bolts teaching and training, new distributor orientation on up to mini local, regional business building seminars and major national and international events. We think locally, regionally, nationally and internationally. It is expected of everyone to look at the calendar grid and to attend as many functions as possible, to invite everyone they work with so everyone can work as a team.

Direct Selling 105

This industry was built door to door and in livings rooms, in the streets and small nutrition shops or mini warehouses around the world. It was built by the person next door talking to you about a great product they are selling and a business opportunity to help you become free to live the life you have dreamed of. Direct selling began with one person talking to another belly to belly. It has been that way for over the past 100 years and will continue that way.

However, we live in a new age. Social Networking, as worn out as that term is, is here to stay and forever changed the way we sell, interact, date, buy things, communicate and has become a way of life for many. Direct selling will always be a person to person business but the rules are changing. Most Micro Entrepreneurs have their own web sites, Facebook pages or fill stadiums to reach people, to build and interact with their community and of course create their own Community Commerce engine. But still the Internet has not become what it can be for direct selling. It certainly has for eBay.

People have products and services they are selling to people they know and others around the world they will never meet, via the Internet, every minute of every day. Guess what? There are a few billion that are not online and every Internet company is trying to figure out how to change that. But the reality is there will always be a countless number of people unplugged especially those that need this industry more than anything else to break the cycle of hopelessness and poverty. This is the power of direct selling — it is both Online and offline — and either way or together it works.

Reaching a few hundred million people to empower them to live better and make money just isn't going to happen through the Web alone. Although the Web may be able to enable large groups of people to interact with each other online, very few will ever do anything more but look up information.

The direct selling industry believes belly to belly is the primary way to reach people in this industry and it will likely be that way always. However, the Web is a powerful tool, both negative and positive, for the industry and very few have figured out a business model that really takes advantage of it. How many friends do you have on Facebook? How many LinkedIn contacts do you have? How many contacts in outlook or all over the world on your phone? A few billion if you add everyone's up.

I had a stark realization that direct selling is not just going to be a Facebook page for a distributor but a medium for them to buy products and services and to sign up to be a distributor. The reach is enormous and so is the community that lives next door, in the same town or village or a slum where you be living today. But in order to link these two ways of doing business, if it is possible for you, to be successful as a Micro Entrepreneur in this industry you have to use everything at your disposal. This means meetings, door to door, belly to belly, Facebook, You Tube, Twitter and whatever it takes. If you have a community of people that you have developed as a direct seller it is essential that it is constantly harvested and cared for. Reaching that community regularly will be greatly enhanced using a social media approach in today's world.

So many people I know in this industry just put their ego and their success stories online and expect to inspire people to try to be like them. They preach from stage and show off their planes, trains and automobiles. Yes, this is cool and gets people dreaming. But this sets up almost all people they interact with for failure. It is not just about the cars and boats and trips and jewelry. It is about extra money and freedom and does not matter how little or how much. If you have any more than before you are a success. Many will never reach the level of a very successful industry leader and they just don't need to. Although there are new success stories every single day of people graduating into those multi-millionaire ranks, there are vastly more that are getting a check in the mail every week and feel like failures because they didn't reach a certain level.

Using all the tools I had and not just promoting my success or broadcasting my ego was part of my strategy and my system for *Ultimate Success*. I sought to train and teach people about the business, promote great products and to understand what this industry is all about. It is about changing lives. So I took a whole different approach.

I created an entire support structure behind my community, teaching, training, inspiration, and spiritual healing. I used this powerful medium not just to reach people to get them to buy what I was selling but to keep them involved in the business and engaged with me although I couldn't be with them each day. I used iJot to send video messages out as much as possible to everyone in my organization. I sent emails, tweets, videos, held meetings, I went belly to belly every day and night, filled stadiums, but most of all I gave them the tools they needed. Regardless of what tools you use or how you communicate, there is always an opportunity to spread the word. It may be just one person who gets on board, but you may be very surprised how many will jump into this with you if you use all the tools at your disposal and the way of doing business I am teaching you.

If you look at the Web sites of most companies in the industry it is all about them and their products. But this industry is about you. Although there are always success stories promoted and product information abounds, this just isn't what people are looking for — a hand up — a guide to teach them how to fish — a way out of poverty or a better life. Most every company says "here are my products, here is the business and how to make money doing it and here are all the toys you get if you are successful."

I believe the first thing presented should get you to ask, "why me?" Direct selling is about me. It is me reaching out to you and you to others to fulfill mutual dreams. People want to see others who were once in their position that have become Micro Entrepreneurs so they can immediately relate. Not only do they need to relate to others that have gone before them, they have to understand the industry itself. Jeff Cohen, although new to the business, saw this and recorded 100 video testimonies over a period of 100 days, about Micro Entrepreneurs from every walk of life, to make sure everyone could see themselves in the mirror. Also, the industry has to be a prominent part of everyone's web site. Why? Because it is about them getting into it and building a career and this way a lot of negativity can be overcome. Every company would benefit from this.

Just as explaining and promoting any product or business is essential, promoting a Micro Entrepreneur's business is critical to success. But unless it can speak to the masses, and make it about them, the Internet will not support direct selling as it should. The "why me" is what people are interested in. So much of the Web and information overload is about us or me not them. We have the best products, we are the best people, we offer the best financial advice or legal services or stuff to buy. That is why incremental usage across the Web is so limited, but Facebook is growing bigger than anything. Why? It is about me, we, us and all the above connecting with each other. It is everyone speaking to everyone in a way that creates unity and support. This is where the power lies and anyone getting into the business needs to realize this is a special opportunity and not to bastardize it and make it about their ego. We should make people want to plug in and be warmed to the idea of the industry, the products, the people and the business in a welcoming way.

In my website, I have incorporated all I have learned and the things that can help people even if they didn't sign up to be a distributor. However, at the same time I worked hard to create a

Web experience for people interested in the business and products — both online and offline — that teaches more than simply what I sell. This is the necessary marriage of mediums for direct selling to be successful in this day and age. I know this industry, and my business is about people and helping them grow, prosper, expand their boundaries. That is what helps develop people and win their trust and loyalty. Remember products don't sell products — people do!

Failure is not an Option

Thomas Edison *tried* and failed nearly 2000 *times* and every time learned how not to *make a light bulb,* but he only needed one way to *make* it work. Even with the bad, the struggle or consistent failure you can learn what didn't work and if you keep trying and fighting you will find a way that will work. Failure for some is never an option and doesn't even cross their minds. Failure for them is simply just another step in the process of succeeding. But failure at anything may just be all you need retreat back into yourself and continue to lead your quiet life of desperation. It may be the straw that broke the camel's back for you or you may have lost everything or you are just too scared to try. But I have always said bathe in your failures, wear them proudly and if you are going to fail then fail big. If you cannot stomach the fact that you may not make it regardless of a tireless effort or your perception of failure perhaps coming every step of the way then you will never win big either. "If you don't succeed, then try, try again". Heard that one before? It is at the heart of direct selling.

Direct selling is not a crap shoot. However, most people fail at it. They got into it for a quick hit or thought they were going to get a Lamborghini handed to them in a few months or even three years. They jumped into a company too fast or fell in love with a product. They never really had the perception inside of them that they were starting their own company. They just looked at themselves as a sales person.

A Micro Entrepreneur is not a sales person; he or she is an owner of a real business. And with any business they must buy, sell, do the accounting, pay the bills and yes be prepared to fail and some to fail often. It may take three months or three years to be very successful in this business. Along the way, the majority of those who try direct selling feel like a failure or believe they just aren't good enough at it because they did not advance to a new status in the company or get the dream car. They walk away. Or they have heard many others talk about direct selling or have the perception in their head that it is a bad business to be in so they don't even take the chance that it may be exactly what they need.

My advice to you is if you hear anyone talking about how they walked away because they failed, just don't be like them. Follow *successful* people and surround yourself with them. Ask questions of successful mothers and learn how they handle their everyday lives. Find role models like successful teachers or doctors or first responders or those who have climbed out of poverty. Direct selling is comprised of every single type of person from every background imaginable. You are like thousands doing it I assure you. Follow those who have success in its many forms, not those who want to throw water on a fire before it ever lights in your belly. Do not listen to failures that did not try, try again. And if you feel like one, for whatever reason, then don't live in your head telling yourself you failed. Get out there and do it again until the light bulb lights up. No matter what the cost, what the sacrifice or what the dream is — go for it and be all in — as my friends say "Go Large or Go Home".

The perception of failure, fear of failure and actually failing is what stops so many people in direct selling from being successful. They simply stop! They stop believing in themselves instead of knowing that failure is just part of the game in direct selling and in life. They stop believing in their dream of independence and financial freedom and decide to go back to their former life and shop only to line some company's pockets instead of theirs.

And the best of all, if you already have a job, wouldn't it be great to tell your boss "Take this job and shove it?" That alone for many would be a dream come true!

This career, part time or full time, brings you close to people in a way that no other industry even approaches. It provides people support from the top down and sideways. The relationships I have built, and the ones you will build, will last a lifetime and create a network of people, who at their core want to help. Help is not mandatory in the business but almost everyone jumps in with two feet to help you overcome life issues, business issues and personal issues. The support you will get can change everything for you, but you have to follow through. Then you will quickly find yourself doing this for others, too.

GETTING PERSONAL

Success for people around the world is not just material things. It is about the way they feel and the happiness they can have if they are given a chance. Everyone, no matter where they live and under what circumstances, needs help not just financially but internally. Growing from the inside out is critical to achieving success in any facet of life. Starting your own business may be one the hardest things anyone can do, especially if your situation is dire. This is why it is so important to get personal with you and pass along some advice and wisdom I have gathered over the years. If I can help you be better, be a better person and to grow, then the business you build will grow with you.

Life 101

My inspiration comes from helping others, so I want to provide you a few pointers. It is essential to understand ways to change how you think and feel and learn about the essential building blocks that result in success or failure.

We all have dreams, but very few realize them. Lack of discipline is one major reason, but lack of follow-through is the most prevalent. Many people just want a chance and many more around the world would jump at the chance to be better, be more and to live a freer more fulfilling life.

Follow-through in life is essential. Half measures will only create mediocrity and for you a life less lived. Many have heard "Carpe Diem" — seize the day, you had better believe that is true. Try to think for a moment how your tombstone will read or how you think you will be remembered or noted for what you did with the very short time you spent on this earth. Have you done everything that you desired, could have or should have? No! Will your family be at your bedside in the hospital or miss you when you are gone, or have you alienated them and mistreated that precious relationship? Have you withdrawn, only to sit on the couch and watch TV for hours each day or play on the computer? Almost every single person on our planet isn't living the life they wanted, many never will, and frankly, many can't.

Most people live life day in and day out, escaping into a happy place inside their head. They look for any way out, but do not have the willpower or discipline to change the life they are living because their life, frankly, is not their own. There is somebody else telling them what to do, TV and magazines telling them how to look and feel, people around them telling them they can't or will never make it, but mostly it is their own incorrect beliefs about themselves. You have to be free before you can succeed. This is the most worthy reason for you to become a Micro Entrepreneur.

Many of you reading this may think you have already shattered your dreams or have no hope in ever achieving them, so you give up. You say wishful thinking or I could never do that. Most have even just lost hope and don't dream anymore at all. But if you shoot for the moon you may find yourself flying very high. If you crash and burn but you are still alive then good you live to fight another day. "Whatever doesn't kill you makes you stronger". The opposite of going for it and no matter what trying to live your dream is to continue to live a half measured life and many regrets. You do not want to go to the grave with that I assure you.

Imagine Bill Gates or Mark Zuckerberg staying at Harvard, or Steve Jobs, Henry Ford, Gorbachev, Regan, Waleed, Mandela or Gandhi giving up. Imagine the mother that didn't have that extra time to sit with her children and read to them, hold them close and nurture their young lives. Imagine yourself. What is your dream? Do you even have one? The biggest question is what are you going to do about it? If you can imagine it and work hard, you can do anything your mind becomes set on.

Einstein said something profound "Imagination is more important than knowledge." He also said, by the way, "there are two things that are infinite; the universe and human stupidity." What are you thinking and where do you sit in life as you are reading this? Can you first start with imagining a better life for yourself? Is it stupid to dream? No! Just like every question is a good one. Ask yourself this — "Am I just living a life or living my dream?" You can lie to yourself and that will get you absolutely nowhere, but if you say you are living your dream, then you are one of the very few.

The difference between just living and living your dream is if you are just living, you didn't go for it. Perhaps you were afraid it was too risky to try or simply lacked the self-confidence to go that extra mile which could have made all the difference in the world. Instead of a touchdown or going to the World Cup you punted or bunted and accepted where you were in life and became complacent. If you tried to make your dream come true and didn't make it, then like most, you gave up and retreated back into a life you never really wanted. But more likely is you didn't follow through, reach far enough, work hard enough or didn't have a plan to achieve what you imagined yourself to be.

Of all these, the key is a plan and knowing the rules of the game so that you will not get off track, defocus your efforts, cause yourself failure or spend one minute more of your time in quiet desperation or without hope. Direct selling already has a plan to follow and way of building dreams so that part of your success equation can be consumed and followed by you to achieve success.

"Be all you can be." Billy and I say this as former military men.

Life 102

Are you Surviving in Life, or Living the Dream?

I am not saying you are stupid, fat, dumb and lazy. You may be skinny, beautiful, smart and lazy. You may be demoralized and hopeless, poor beyond measure, or hungry today and every day. But this doesn't mean you have to be. Life changes and can change immensely if you take a dream, any dream, and follow through with discipline to attain it. It starts with a goal and a plan to achieve it. Direct selling is a proven, credible way to do so, with a plan already in place if you follow it.

I ask everyone I know to put words or pictures on their mirror, refrigerator, yacht, car, rickshaw, cubicle, rice bowl or wherever you can stick your dream reminder. It could be buying a car. It could be your child going to college. It could be a picture of me with a bull's eye on it. Who knows? What I do know is that dreams can become reality. But one thing is for sure, if you don't dream, it will never happen and if you continue to do the same things you are doing now you will get the same results. I can help you understand the things that can limit your dreams and cause failure along the way. I can help you to try something different and think in new ways. Just remember, no matter where you go — there you are, and whatever got you here — won't get you there!

It Starts with Today

What about those extra pounds? Did you grab another doughnut last night or decide you would skip a workout or far worse? Did

122

you say "I can't" so you do nothing at all? What if for the next 60 days you worked out each day? It would be an amazing transformation mentally, physically and emotionally. What if you could go 60 days and not tell one lie or save $5 a day, or quit drinking, smoking or drugs? In 60 days, you can begin the foundation of new positive habits.

What if changing today could lead to saving your life? What if you said, "today I am going to get up and take control of who I am and my own destiny." To look in the mirror and say "enough is enough, I am going to change" is *not* enough, but it is the very first step. With change comes struggle, hard work and an unwavering commitment to follow through. If you are willing to commit for the next 60 days to changing your life, then that is what I am talking about. And if you are willing to commit for the next year to using direct selling as a tool; even part-time, or an hour a day to earn extra money, or perhaps even become full time self-employed, then sign up.

Don't just dream it — live it!

If you want to change your life then I can help and direct selling can too. I am not just speaking to you about being successful, I am trying to help you be successful and *stay* successful. I am certain of it and have experienced this with thousands, that when you have a dream, a focus, a goal, you *feel more intense and alive* than the day before you started to go for it. Trust me, the day you decide to get up and really do something about the things you want for yourself and family and build a life like the one you pictured you would have, is the day your perceptions of everything around you will change and perception will become your new reality.

However ambitious your goals and dreams are and however fast and furious you begin to wake up and start making them happen, most people will stop at one point or another. "I'm too tired" or "I don't feel good" or "I'll never be able to do this — what was I thinking?" They become demoralized and feel like failures when all they had to do is push themselves an extra hour or two that day and they would have made it to another day. Even if the next day the same things go through your mind; I can't, I won't, I don't feel like it or I don't have time, just look at your dream picture or an entire dream board, your children, spouse or family and remember one more day is all the difference in the world.

Life 103

It is all in your mind. We all have dreams and want desperately to achieve them, but most don't have the will or even have a plan to help make them come true. Their dreams, hopes and goals are traded for a couch and TV, another day at the office doing a job they hate, or perhaps the daily grind of finding food or water to live. Their dreams, those ambitious thoughts, evaporate back into their minds. Instead of doing something, many just live out the glory days in their mind and never even try to make today the first day they will actually try to do something to make their dreams come true.

People stop believing that dreams can happen to them too, so they accept only imagining themselves living a dream, being a rock star on stage or a rich and powerful person instead of actually doing something to really make their dreams become reality. I am not saying that just anyone can be a rock star, a movie star or professional athlete for example, but I am saying you can be much more than you are today. The very first thing is you MUST get out of living in your own head and get out of your own way.

You have to take what is up in that brain of yours and start doing something positive about it.

Worse than just playing reruns in your mind or fantasizing about things or people, is the playing out of terrible scenarios on the mind's TV screen. Many, many people play out scenarios of failure or have anxiety about future outcomes. By doing so, they actually set themselves up for failure. As simple as it sounds, speaking positive thoughts to yourself and to others can bring success, not just in business but throughout your life.

The mind is a powerful tool that can have a profound positive or negative impact on each day of your life. Here is a quote from the great French philosopher Montaigne that is one of the most powerful I have read about negative thinking — "My *life* has been full of *terrible misfortunes* most of which never happened". Do you understand the meaning of that? It means that many people, the majority in fact, live out dreams and nightmares in their mind and the mind makes it real. The chemicals released by negative thinking or thinking worst case scenarios is not just mentally damaging it is actually physically damaging as well. You see the mind actually doesn't know the difference from the real life we live and the one we live inside our heads, so it goes into overdrive to protect you from yourself. Although the events never occurred, or the fantasy or dream you played in your mind's eye never really happened, your body and mind's reaction will be the same as if it actually happened.

It is like waking up from a dream that seems real. You feel anxious, sad, depressed if it was a nightmare or elated and excited if it was a good dream. Bad dreams, as well as, bad thoughts cause rushes of chemicals from our brains throughout our bodies and you may not even be aware of them. You may be so used to your rut or wallowing in self-pity that you never recognize the difference it causes. It just goes on day in and day out with sporadic moments of fleeting happiness. If you are like so many that do this then you can alter the path of your life with some simple changes and train your brain to become an engine of positivity and results of happiness, joy and freedom will come.

Life 104

The power of the positive. Regardless of how you wake up or what circumstances you wake up to, it is imperative — absolutely crucial — you think of the positive things the day may bring you. Every single day of your life is precious, but so few of us ever accept this gift and develop the habit of taking it to heart. You can choose today to project failure upon yourself, anger at others or simply remain in a foul mood. Regardless it is you, not anyone else, that feels that way and you are the cause of it.

The hope that there will be a better tomorrow or that today something good will happen, is not the routine of most everyone and certainly not for billions of people around the world. Everyday seems like the last, and tomorrow will be more of the same. People harbor resentment, envy for the greener grass, and non-forgiveness that only burdens them, not the un-forgiven. Many wake up with a grudge, pissed off and moping around just expecting more of the same and the worst to happen. They measure tomorrow by yesterday and forget that today is the key to making sure it is better tomorrow than yesterday or if yesterday was great then they can have more of it tomorrow by doing and thinking the right way today.

There is one thing for sure — you cannot change what happened yesterday, whether it was good or bad. You can only live today in the hope that how you live and look at the day will bring a better tomorrow. Practice makes perfect and practicing the very difficult daily positive outlook right when you wake will make serious changes happen in your life and your plan for success.

Even harder is to always think positively, regardless of what has happened to you. If you start every day with conviction to be a positive person, good things and a renewed feeling of joy will permeate your life. The alternative is you can choose to make yourself feel bad, not anyone else, and be resentful of what happened yesterday or wait for something bad to happen today. Failure, future regret and carrying around the mental trash will be sure to sink your boat and drown your dreams. This is the fundamental flaw and defeatist mentality that poisons a person's drive to be successful as a Micro Entrepreneur or in any business or in life.

I am Positive

This pattern of negative thinking and behavior plagues us all and anyone reading this knows it is true. Negative thinking leads to negative attitudes and negative outcomes. Your mind plays tricks on you, but you play tricks on you much more. People lie to themselves and cheat themselves out of a fuller and freer life hourly. People live out fantasies in their minds that they will never have and live out terrible misfortunes most of which never come true. Many have heard the power of positive thinking or read the book. In every situation there is some good no matter how bad. "Bad things can happen to good people". It is very true. But it is how you accept them that makes all the difference in your life. You can choose to clutter your mind and poison the air around you or you can choose to use whatever the experience is, as a tool to better yourself.

Some things though are not that easy; like a death or physical injury or worse, but you are responsible for moving on no matter how broken you may be — you must persevere for yourself and those that depend on you. Success alone will not cure any brokenness. "Many broken men (and women) drive shinny cars". Being successful, rich and famous isn't going to change the fundamentals of your life. Don't get me wrong, it sure does make doing things more convenient, but all the money in the world isn't going to change your perception of who you are and what life can be regardless of what happens to you. Only you can.

If you don't look at even the worst things as learning experiences or with a positive outlook, I can't help you, this book can't help you and you living inside your mind definitely won't help you. Cursing the darkness is like throwing rocks at the sun or yelling at the jerk that cut you off on the freeway. It does absolutely nothing but cause frustration, anger and resentment for you and only you. Do you think the other guy that cut you off is feeling bad or angry? No — only you are. Do you think the people that wronged you feel like they need to be forgiven to feel good — most likely not. It is you that carries this trash around with you not them. Negative thinking, speaking and dragging the carcass of past doings around with you will equal failure every time. Unless I can help you change these behaviors, even if they don't happen every day, even the freedom, joy and fulfillment direct selling can breathe into your life, won't help one darn bit.

Life 105

Help me help you! The Self Help and Motivation industry is big, just as direct selling is. One thing for sure about the direct selling industry is it is all about people helping people. I tell everyone that this is a people business; it starts with them and ends with them. I do everything in my power to help as many people on earth as I can. The industry just happens to be a vehicle for me to

reach them and help them become free and financially independent. But I have failed at helping many others because I failed to
change their way of thinking about the world around them. Over
the years I have discovered there are some very simple rules and
exercises that if you understand and use will help you in everything you do.

Whenever you start thinking something negative or about
ready to say something negative about someone else — STOP!
Immediately try to remember what you are learning here. Change
the subject in your mind and think of something good if you
can, regardless of how bad what you are thinking is. Try to see
if there is any good that may come of the situation, or how that
person you harbor ill will toward, could become valuable to you
as an ally instead of an enemy. Dale Carnegies' book "*How to
Win Friends and Influence People*" is a must-read and I make sure
everyone in my businesses reads it. There is good in everyone,
although I have found it very hard to find sometimes, and there
is some good that can come from any situation you may find
yourself in or face.

There have been times and will be times that you are going
along and something terrible happens or you think about terrible
things. It is like a beautiful piano being played and one of the
keys gets stuck. The note just keeps playing over and over and
drowns out any good thoughts. In other words, you are stuck.
You are stuck listening to yourself. You fixate on it and live out
the happenings over and over in your head, but nothing will
ever change what has already happened. To get unstuck, you
have to look at things with a different eye. An eye you likely have
never used or barely ever look upon things with. No matter what
happens in life, it is you that chooses to feel good or bad about it.
You choose to be happy or sad. You choose to feel angry or to let

it go. It is happening to you and you only, not to them or the situation. Only you can unstick the piano key, but you have to work at it and try hard to develop the mental fortitude to think positive and be positive and I assure you even the worst of situations will get better.

If you get stuck, I want you to try this mental exercise. Imagine yourself inside your house, or tent or car or wherever you may find yourself. Imagine yourself walking out your door, to the river, or down the road or wherever your path may lead you. Picture yourself and then begin to look from an aerial view down on the forest, your town or city and begin to keep expanding to other places you have seen or other place you want to go. You are almost flying, seeing the world from a different perspective from inside your mind. Moving from one place to another and using your mind to move you is very easy to do. It takes your perception of the actual time and the space you were just in and trades it for another. This simple process can quickly get you unstuck and can change your own mental path, so you don't spiral further into your thoughts.

If you are anxious about something that may happen in the future, as most of us are from time to time, you can help yourself too. There are many scenarios one plays out inside their heads and most of them bad. This leads those chemicals to travel throughout your body and the lingering thoughts to stay in your head. Think of the worst thing that can happen. The very worst is what you should picture for yourself. It can be very bad even horrible if it actually happens. But accept it and own it. Be prepared for the very worst and get comfortable with it. This is the very worst thing that can happen. Once you can see the very worst you can begin to plan how it can be fixed, taken advantage of or what will come next. Getting comfortable with a worst case scenario is a way to quiet your mind, get back to thinking positively and get back to focusing on success. This exercise has worked for me and many others I have taught. If you find yourself anxious and worried then this is the best way to help yourself get out of your own way.

Positive thinking, positive speaking and having the hope that you can create a better future can make a huge difference in your life and your success. One of the Cardinal Rules of this industry and any other facet of your life is to always speak positively about people, businesses and even circumstance even though they may not all be deserving of it. If you speak and think negatively about someone or something, it is likely to haunt you and come back amplified. Ultimately, no good can come from it. Applying that brainpower in a positive way will, I absolutely know it, change the everyday outcomes you will have and is the most important factor for success in this industry.

To change your circumstances and be successful in a people business like direct selling, you must first influence your own thinking. The mind is powerful and the key to success in any business and life. Try this. Sit and think of an apple. Think of nothing else but the apple for five minutes. You will see that you can't keep your mind from flashing thoughts through your head or other thoughts coming into your mind. I bet in the first 10 seconds it happened to you. This shows us that how little control we have over our thoughts. This why you have to work hard every day to think positively, do positive things and plan each day so that positive things can happen to you.

Do you wake up and look in that mirror and look away simply because you don't like what you see? Or are you someone that simply can't stand going off to the job that owns you, facing the family who doesn't know you, the marriage that isn't working for you, the hope that isn't there or just another day living in the skin that holds you back? You can look at yourself and lie or be honest with yourself and change it. You can rant and rave and continue to throw rocks at the sun or you can begin to open new doors. You can surround yourself with the same people or find new ones that are more inspiring and uplifting. Most of all, it is within your power to create or recreate who you are, change your perception about circumstances and fly high above the trees.

Get Busy Living or Get Busy Dying!

WHY NOT YOU, WHY NOT NOW

Some of you may have read my recent book "*Why Not You, Why Not Now*." I am certain it will benefit you in your own journey toward success and perhaps help you follow in the footsteps of others like me who have made direct selling a lucrative career. The solutions outlined in this book, or any other, mean nothing if you do not wake up, look at yourself in the mirror and do something about it.

If you follow Jesus like me or even know of him, you can understand the impact one can have on billions. He sponsored twelve people and invested three and a half years teaching and training them. They in turn reached a few who reached a few and so on until now the whole world has been reached. Although none of us might ever have that impact, there comes great power in helping others to understand how they can better themselves then help others in return. No matter where you live in the world, Micro Entrepreneurship can change your life, like it has mine. If it can change your life then you can change other people's lives too. It is a snowball effect and why I believe the world needs this solution desperately.

Taking a look at the world and its many problems from a perspective of jobs is not a mainstream consideration. People do not realize the power of a job and powerlessness of not having one. This issue all around the world and the primary drivers of it are full of misconceptions and lack of understanding, as is the case with direct selling.

If you have ever traveled overseas, or even throughout America, you have witnessed the economic hopelessness firsthand, and after you have read this book, I am hopeful you understand the cause. This world is desperate for change and desperate for liberty. There is no better accomplishment than to help someone take charge of their own destiny.

Be it overthrowing a government, economic collapse, hopelessness, chronic poverty, starvation and other deeply disconcerting issues the world faces, the underlying cause is lack of economic hope and prosperity. The larger the base of citizens in the world that are middle class or have a means of one day becoming part of it, the more the dangers we face from war and terrorism are reduced. You may find it very unusual that I have suggested direct selling as an antidote to war or terrorism, but the fact is, the world needs businesses to employ people; without jobs, nations can be overthrown and the ground becomes more fertile to enlist those that mean others harm. All the governments, with their borrowing and subsidies, and every company in the world, have no means to solve it. That is simply impossible given the size and scale of the issue. Without a model that can spread like wildfire and graduate people into an economically valuable part of the food chain, this whole thing can collapse.

I am not an alarmist, I am an optimist. But, I cannot remain optimistic when I see the world's poverty and hopelessness both on TV every night and firsthand. I have looked topographically at the world we live in and I am compelled to do something about it, albeit a small part of the greater effort. This book is just the beginning of my crusade.

I have been very surprised at the response and the warm reception direct selling is receiving from leaders across the world, in both industry and politics. I was fearful that the reputation of the industry, that we all know proceeds it, would thwart my goals out of the gate and frankly, it almost did. I overcame many objections but ultimately once I explained the industry and the power it holds, with the help of Billy Glynn, those misperceptions quickly faded.

I am truly a fisher of men and woman. My only true fulfillment comes from helping others and a hope that one might even change the world someday or just change their lives and the lives of their family for the better. I look at things differently now from when I couldn't pay the electric bill, and see the world in a whole new light. In order for me to light a candle, not curse the darkness, it was necessary to present the industry and this opportunity to you in a different way. But more so, to teach that direct selling is a powerful and transformational way for you to look at things differently too.

I always try to look for the good in everything. With all that the world faces, now and in the future, and the challenges you may have in your life, I am positive that Micro Entrepreneurship is the key to success. You have the tools to change, and the world has at least one it can unleash. I am hopeful that you can use what you have learned about Micro Entrepreneurship and help me make the world a better place. It is one person changing one person at a time; I for one hope I can continue to challenge both the industry and you to change for the better and to live a life of purpose and prosperity.

Take Action

> *"Action expresses priorities". "An ounce of practice*
> *is worth more than tons of preaching".*
> Mahatma Gandhi

A Micro Entrepreneur wants to learn how to fish. They do not want a hand out they want the tools and training to be self-sufficient for life. They want a hand up. They do not look to others or the government to feed them or subsidize them. They do not put their hand out and say give me more and more. They want freedom and have the willpower to achieve it. There are millions of small, medium and large business owners that have done the same and who fight for their liberty and "Gainful Self-Employment" every day. Micro Entrepreneurs and traditional entrepreneurs all share one thing in common. They pick up their rod and go fishing.

Others have a job and like robots just live day in and day out on the corporate treadmill. They have a fishing rod too but it is attached to their back with a pay check on the hook dangling in front of their face. They run and run after the next promotion and wait for the next pay day even though they may hate what they do, or are simply like drones programmed to work their lives away for someone else.

Others want a hand out. They want to be handed something and return expect to do nothing for it. They are dependent on others, particularly governments, for their sustenance and do not have the willpower or even the desire to change. This is the mentality of entitlement and socialism that pervades many societies on earth. They expect fish to be handed to them day in and day out and feel no guilt or shame in it.

Finally, there are those who want desperately to change and better themselves. They want a chance but may never have one. The statistics do not lie. They have no hope. They live in fear and desperation. They have no way out. These are the billions I speak of and within their ranks, if given the opportunity to get a hand up, they would likely bite into this opportunity and never let go.

If you are one of the tens of millions that want to change their lives then follow the plan the direct selling industry has for you. If you are willing to take the next step, then take my advice; get in and get started. Direct selling will help you live a healthier, happier and more prosperous lifestyle...not to mention the pure fun you will have by helping others to succeed. Direct selling can be a whole new way of life for you whether you are already in, getting in or decide to be all in.

Those of us who are already in will hand you a fishing pole and teach you how to use it. When you get in make sure to follow what is being taught and remember the following:

- Define your dream — Daily
- Develop a *PMA*: *Positive Mental Attitude* by reading listening and participating
- Work like it depends on you and pray like it depends on God
- Never quit
- Plan your work, and work your plan
- Stay connected to leaders in your organization
- Build width for profitability and depth for stability
- Never stop sponsoring personally
- Do not give unsolicited information
- Stay consistent and persistent doing the activities that pay: Sponsoring people and moving product
- KISS: Keep it Super Simple
- Learn to become a good financial steward of your resources: You manage not someone else
- Give, Give, Give, Give then Give some more
- Dream big and give it away
- Promote, Promote, Promote, Promote

The simple truth is if you are looking for a hand up and not a hand out then the best place to look is at the end of your own arm. You have a candle in hand now and it is up to you light it and to pass it on to others.

WORKS CITED

1. **World Bank.** *World Bank Development Indicators.* 2008.
2. **Ravallion, Shaohua Chen and Martin.** *The developing World is Poorer Than We Thought, But No Less Successful in the Fight Against Poverty,.* s.l. : World Bank, 2008.
3. **UNICEF.** *The State of the World's Children — Fact Sheet.* 1999.
4. **United Nations Development Program.** *Human Development Report.* s.l. : Palgrave Macmillan, 2006.
5. **International Energy Agency.** *Electric Access Database.* 2009.
6. **UNICEF.** *State of the World's Children.* 2005.
7. **New Internationalist.** *State of the World Report — Issue 287.* 1997, New Internationalist Magazine.
8. **Schawbel, Dan.** Gallup's Jim Clifton on The Coming Jobs War. *Forbes.* October 26, 2011.
9. **International Labour Office.** *Global Employment Trends for Youth — Special issue on the impace of te global economic crisis on youth.* 2010.
10. **US Department of Agriculture.** *Supplemental Nutrition Assistance Program Participation and Costs.* 2012.
11. **US Census Bureau.** *Income, Poverty, and Health Insurance Coverage in the United States.* 2010.
12. **Hipple, Steven F.** *Self-employment in the US.* s.l. : Division of Labor Force Statistics, Bureau of Labor Statistics, 2009.
13. **Bureau of Labor Statistics.** Consumer Expenditures 2010. *Economic News Release.* 2011.
14. **Riedl, Brian.** *Heritage Foundation.* 2010.

15. **IRS.** *Individual Income Tax Returns with Positive Adjusted Gross Income (AGI) Returns Classified by Tax Percentile — Early Release.* 2009.

16. **US Central Intelligence Agency.** *The World Fact Book.* 2011.

17. **Tax Policy Center.** *Baseline Distribution of Tax Units with No Income Tax Liability by Cash Income Percentile.* 2011.

18. **Labonte, Marc.** *The Economic Implications of the Long-Term Federal Budget Outlook.* s.l. : http://aging.senate.gov/crs/medicare8.pdf, 2010.

19. **US Central Intelligence Agency.** *The World Factbook.* 2012.

20. **The Heritage Foundation.** *Index of Economic Freedom.* 2012.

21. **Gallop.** *Gallop Student Poll — US Overall Data.* 2011.

22. **Direct Selling Association.** *Direct Selling 411.* [Online] http://www.directselling411.com/about-this-site/.

23. *Top 50 Direct Selling Companies by Sales Volume.* **Direct Selling Magazine.** 2011.

APPENDIX A

Below is a list of the top 50 companies as published by the *Direct Selling News* in 2011. Again, this is a testament to the importance of the magazine.

Many companies on the list have increased in size while others have trailed off in revenue and some substantially. These are based on 2009 revenues and are meant to demonstrate the size and maturity of the industry only. [23]

1. Avon Products, Inc.
2010 Revenue: $10.9 billion
Country: USA
2009 Revenue: $10.3 billion
Compensation Plan: Single-level and multi-level
Products: Beauty, fashion jewelry and apparel
Distributors: 6.5 million

2. Amway
2010 Revenue: $9.2 billion
Country: USA
2009 Revenue: $8.4 billion
Compensation Plan: Multi-level
Products: Nutrition, beauty, personal-care and home-care products
Distributors: 3 million

3. Natura Cosmeticos SA
2010 Revenue: $3 billion
Country: Brazil
2009 Revenue: $2.4 billion
Compensation Plan: Bi-level
Products: Personal-care products and fragrances
Distributors: 1 million

4. Vorwerk & Co. KG
2010 Revenue: $2.9 billion
Country: Germany
2009 Revenue: $3.5 billion
Compensation Plan: Multi-level (JAFRA Cosmetics)
Products: Cosmetics and home appliances
Distributors: 600,000

5. Herbalife Ltd.
2010 Revenue: $2.7 billion
Country: USA
2009 Revenue: $2.3 billion
Compensation Plan: Multi-level
Products: Nutritional supplements; health/fitness, wellness, skin- and hair-care; and weight-management products
Distributors: 2.1 million

6. Mary Kay Inc.
2010 Revenue: $2.5 billion
Country: USA
2009 Revenue: $2.5 billion
Compensation Plan: Single-level and multi-level
Products: Skin-care products and color cosmetics

7. Tupperware Brands Corp.
2010 Revenue: $2.3 billion
Country: USA
2009 Revenue: $2.1 billion
Compensation Plan: Single-level and multi-level
Products: Storage and serving products; beauty- and personal-care products
Distributors: 2.6 million

8. Oriflame Cosmetics S.A.
2010 Revenue: $2.2 billion
Country: Sweden
2009 Revenue: $1.8 billion
Compensation Plan: Multi-level
Products: Beauty products
Distributors: 3.5 million

9. Forever Living Products
2010 Revenue: $1.7 billion
Country: USA
2009 Revenue: $1.7 billion
Compensation Plan: Multi-level
Distributors: 9.3 million

10. Nu Skin Enterprises, Inc.
2010 Revenue: $1.5 billion
Country: USA
2009 Revenue: $1.3 billion
Compensation Plan: Multi-level
Products: Personal care and nutritional products
Distributors: 800,000

11. Belcorp/L'Bel Paris
2010 Revenue: $1.3 billion
Country: Peru
2009 Revenue: $1 billion
Compensation Plan: Single-level and multi-level
Products: Skin-care, fragrance, makeup, body-care, hair-care
Distributors: 840,000

11. Primerica Inc.
2010 Revenue: $1.3 billion
Country: USA
2009 Revenue: $2.2 billion
Compensation Plan: Multi-level
Products: Financial services

13. Miki Corporation
2010 Revenue: $927 million
Country: Japan
2009 Revenue: $969 million
Products: Foods, cosmetics and household products

14. Ignite Inc.
2010 Revenue: $902 million
Country: USA

2009 Revenue: $845 million
Compensation Plan: Multi-level
Products: Electricity and natural gas
Distributors: 195,199

15. Melaleuca Inc.

2010 Revenue: $750 million
Country: USA
2009 Revenue: $879 million
Compensation Plan: Single-level
Products: Personal-care products, cosmetics, cleaning supplies and vitamins

15. Omnilife

2010 Revenue: $750 million
Country: Mexico
2009 Revenue: $750 million
Compensation Plan: Multi-level
Products: Nutritional supplements, weight-management and beauty products, beverages, cosmetics and fragrances
Distributors: 5 million

17. MonaVie LLC

2010 Revenue: $600 million
Country: USA
2009 Revenue: $785 million
Compensation Plan: Multi-level
Products: Foods and nutritional products
Distributors: 1 million

17. Telecom Plus

2010 Revenue: $600 million
Country: United Kingdom
2009 Revenue: $590 million‡
Compensation Plan: Multi-level
Products: Landline phones, broadband, mobile phones, gas, electricity
Distributors: 30,000

17. Yanbal International/Unique
2010 Revenue: $600 million
Country: Peru
2009 Revenue: $490 million
Compensation Plan: Multi-level
Products: Skin-care products, personal-care products, cosmetics, jewelry and fragrances
Distributors: 350,000

20. ACN
2010 Revenue: $553 million
Country: USA
2009 Revenue: $553 million
Compensation Plan: Multi-level
Products: Telecommunications, home services and business services

21. PartyLite (Blyth)
2010 Revenue: $545 million
Country: USA
2009 Revenue: $621.6 million
Compensation Plan: Multi-level
Products: Candles, candle warmers, flameless fragrance, home accents, personal-care products and food products
Distributors: 63,556

22. Amore Pacific
2010 Revenue: $539 million
Country: South Korea
2009 Revenue: $475 million
Products: Cosmetics, personal-care, health products and tea products
Distributors: Not available

23. LG Household & Health Care
2010 Revenue: $532 million
Country: South Korea
2009 Revenue: $461 million‡
Compensation Plan: Not available
Products: Cosmetics and household products

24. USANA Health Sciences Inc.
2010 Revenue: $517 million
Country: USA
2009 Revenue: $436.9 million
Compensation Plan: Multi-level
Products: Nutritional supplements, personal-care, energy and weight-management products
Distributors: 228,000

25. Shaklee Corp.
2010 Revenue: $500 million
Country: USA
2009 Revenue: $500 million
Compensation Plan: Multi-level
Products: Nutritional supplements, skin-care, weight management, green cleaners
Distributors: 1.25 million

25. The Pampered Chef Ltd.
2010 Revenue: $500 million
Country: USA
2009 Revenue: $500 million
Compensation Plan: Multi-level
Products: High-end tools for cooking and entertaining
Distributors: 60,000

25. Tiens/Tianshi
2010 Revenue: $500 million
Country: China
2009 Revenue: $275 million
Compensation Plan: Uni-level and breakaway
Products: Wellness products, dietary supplements

28. Pre-Paid Legal Services, Inc.
2010 Revenue: $454 million
Country: USA
2009 Revenue: $458 million
Compensation Plan: Multi-level
Products: Legal consultation services
Distributors: 425,000

29. Tahitian Noni International, Inc.
2010 Revenue: $420 million
2009 Revenue: $450 million
Compensation Plan: Multi-level
Products: Noni-based drinks, supplements, skin-care, hair-care
Distributors: 500,000

30. Market America Inc.
2010 Revenue: $416 million
Country: USA
2009 Revenue: $284 million
Compensation Plan: Single-level
Products: Health and nutrition, anti-aging, cosmetics, personal-care, weight management, financial services, home and garden, pet care, telecommunications, Internet, auto care
Distributors: 180,000

31. Ambit Energy, L.P.
2010 Revenue: $415 million
Country: USA
2009 Revenue: $324 million
Compensation Plan: Multi-level
Products: Energy
Distributors: 100,000

32. WIV Wein Int'l AG
2010 Revenue: $385 million
Country: Germany
2009 Revenue: $385 million‡
Compensation Plan: Not available
Products: Wines
Distributors: 4,000

33. Scentsy
2010 Revenue: $382 million
Country: USA
2009 Revenue: $178 million
Compensation Plan: Multi-level
Products: Wickless candles, ceramic warmers and fragrance products
Distributors: 105,000

34. Pola Inc.
2010 Revenue: $361 million
Country: Japan
2009 Revenue: $400 million
Compensation Plan: Single-level
Products: Cosmetics, skin-care, personal-care and nutritional products, fashion and jewelry
Distributors: 120,000

35. Arbonne International Inc.
2010 Revenue: $357 million
Country: USA
2009 Revenue: $370 million
Compensation Plan: Multi-level
Products: Skin-care, color cosmetics, nutrition, aromatherapy
Distributors: 600,000+

36. FORDAYS Co. Ltd.
2010 Revenue: $350 million
Country: Japan
2009 Revenue: $344 million
Products: Nutritional

37. Nature's Sunshine Products Inc.
2010 Revenue: $349 million
Country: USA
2009 Revenue: $343 million
Compensation Plan: Multi-level
Products: Aromatherapy, nutritional supplements and skin-care products
Distributors: 685,000

38. NOEVIR Co., Ltd.
2010 Revenue: $345 million
Country: Japan
2009 Revenue: $613 million
Compensation Plan: Single-level
Products: Skin-care, body-care, nutritional supplements and cosmetics
Distributors: 180,000

39. Southwestern
2010 Revenue: $337 million
Country: USA
Compensation Plan: Multi-level
Products: Family-oriented educational reference books and software
Distributors: 2,800

40. KK ASSURAN
2010 Revenue: $333 million
Country: Japan
2009 Revenue: $375 million
Compensation Plan: Multi-level
Products: Skin-care
Distributors: 500,000

41. LR Health & Beauty Systems
2010 Revenue: $307 million
Country: Germany
2009 Revenue: $295 million
Compensation Plan: Multi-level
Products: Well-being and beauty products and supplements, jewelry and luxury items
Distributors: 300,000

42. Aerus Holdings Inc. LLC
2010 Revenue: $300 million
Country: USA
2009 Revenue: $300 million
Compensation Plan: Single-level hybrid and multi-level
Products: Vacuum cleaners, air purifiers, cleansers, allergy control products, nutritional supplements and electronic equipment
Distributors: 35,000

42. Sunrider
2010 Revenue: $300 million
Country: USA
2009 Revenue: $462 million
Compensation Plan: Multi-level

Products: Food and nutritional products, personal care and household products
Distributors: 300,000

44. Cosway

2010 Revenue: $298 million
Country: Malaysia
2009 Revenue: $225 million
Compensation Plan: Retail/multi-level hybrid
Products: Supplements, skin-care, personal-care, cosmetics, household products, car care, food items and lingerie

45. Eureka Forbes Ltd.

2010 Revenue: $272 million
Country: India
2009 Revenue: $272 million
Compensation Plan: 60% fixed/40% variable
Products: Water purifiers, vacuum cleaners, security and industrial systems
Distributors: 25,200

46. Isagenix International

2010 Revenue: $256 million
Country: USA
2009 Revenue: $245 million
Compensation Plan: Binary multi-level
Products: Nutritional cleansing and replenishing products as well as skin-care, anti-aging and weight-management products
Distributors: 25,000

47. Neways, Inc.

2010 Revenue: $250 million
Country: USA
2009 Revenue: $400 million
Compensation Plan: Multi-level
Products: Nutritional, personal care and household products
Distributors: 350,000

49. Vivint, Inc.
2010 Revenue: $245 million
Country: USA/Canada
Compensation Plan: Not available
Products: Home automation, energy management and residential security

50. Charle Corp. Ltd.
2010 Revenue: $240 million
Country: Japan
Charle Corporation Ltd. is a Japan-based company, principally engaged in the wholesale of women's undergarments. The company sells its products through distributors through home parties, specialty stores and agent stores.
2009 Revenue: $200 million
Compensation Plan: Not available
Products: Women's lingerie, cosmetics

50. KOYO-SHA
2010 Revenue: $240 million
Country: Japan
2009 Revenue: $291 million
Compensation Plan: Multi-level
Products: Nutritional supplements, cosmetics and personal-care products
Distributors: 300,000

APPENDIX B

Amounts shown are *monthly residual income 2010 of some of the most successful direct selling professionals.*

1. Lita & Brig Hart Monavie $950,000 www.brighart.com
2. Barry Chi & Holly Chen Amway $850,000 www.amway.com
3. Howe Kean & Shu Chen Foo Amway $450,000 www.amway.com
4. Enrique & Graciela Varela Herbalife $425,000 www.herbalife.com
5. Gina & Steve Merritt Monavie $407,000 www.Monavie.com
6. Carol & Ken Porter Monavie $400,000 www.Monavie.com
7. Sunny Su & Debra Hsu Hsieh Amway $400,000 www.envip.com/en.asp
8. Charlie & Debbie Kalb Monavie $398,000 www.Monavie.com
9. Rolf Kipp Forever Living Products $375,000 www.flp-europe.com
10. Mike Dillard Magnetic Sponsoring $365,000 www.mikedillard.net/blog
11. Bill & Peggy Britt Amway $350,000 www.bww.com
12. Dexter Yager Amway $350,000 www.dexandbirdieyager.com
13. George Zalucki & Art Napolitano ACN $350,000 www.georgezalucki.com
14. Jim & Nancy Dornan Amway $350,000 www.n21corp.com
15. Max Schwarz Amway $350,000 www.schwarz-organisation.eu
16. Peter & Eva Muller-Meerkatz Amway $350,000 www.peterundevamm.com
17. Sharon & Steven Sharif Xango $350,000 www.shariffamily.com
18. Tsuyoshi Tomioka Synergy $350,000 www.synergyworldwide.com
19. Jay Kubassek CarbonCopyPro $300,000 www.carboncopypro.com
20. John Peterson Herbalife $300,000 www.herbalife.com
21. Kaoru Nakajima Amway $300,000 www.heckel.ne.jp
22. Marco & Milagro Dubon Forever Living Products $300,000 www.foreverliving.com
23. Susan Peterson Herbalife $300,000 www.herbalife.com
24. Darrell & Tracy Utterbach Monavie $292,000 www.Monavie.com
25. Kelly Bangert Monavie $292,000 www.kellybangert.com
26. Onyx Coale Monavie $292,000 www.onyxcoale.com

27. Ron & Brenda Prudhomme Monavie $292,000 www.Monavie.com
28. Scott & Sue Olsen Monavie $292,000 www.Monavie.com
29. Corbin & Holly Roush Monavie $270,168 www.Monavie.com
30. Steve & Melyn Campbell Exfuze $252,000 www.soupynetwork.com
31. Dave Johnson Nikken $250,000 www.nikken.com
32. Debbie & Geoff Davis ACN $250,000 www.ACNinc.com
33. Jeff Roberti NSA-Juiceplus $250,000 www.roberti.net
34. Kang Hyeon Sook & Ryu InIk Amway $250,000 www.amway.com
35. Leonard & Esther Kim Amway $250,000 www.wwdbkorea.com
36. Mark & Peggy Lei Amway $250,000 www.amway.com
37. Roberto Ruiz For Ever Living Products $250,000 www.foreverliving.com
38. Simon Abboud ACN $250,000 www.ACNinc.com
39. Adrian Eimerl & Shawn Herrick & Jeremy Rose ACN $240,000 www.ACNinc.com
40. Leonard & Esther Kim Amway $225,000 www.amway.com
41. Shane & Dana Douglas ACN $225,000 www.ACNinc.com
42. Carol & Alan Lorrenz Herbalife $220,000 www.herbalife.com
43. Mathieu Lamontagne ACN $220,000 www.ACNinc.com
44. Patrick Maser & Mike Maser ACN $215,000 www.ACNinc.com
45. Danny Bae ACN $210,000 www.ACNinc.com
46. Jeff Weber ACN $205,000 www.ACNinc.com
47. Domo Kovacevic ACN $204,000 www.ACNinc.com
48. Mike Bisutti ACN $203,000 www.ACNinc.com
49. Nathan Goldberg ACN $202,000 www.ACNinc.com
50. Brian & Andrea Sax ACN $200,000 www.ACNinc.com

APPENDIX C

Not everyone is the average American family. What matters is your budget. Take a moment and do something that will enlighten you. Take a look at what you make and what you spend in a year not matter where you live on earth.

Food   _____
Housing   _____
Apparel   _____
Transportation   _____
Healthcare   _____
Entertainment   _____
Cash Contributions   _____
Personal Insurance /Pensions _____
Other   _____

What is your total?   _____
Now,
What is your income?   _____
But,
What were your federal taxes last year?   _____
What were your state taxes last year?   _____
What about real-estate taxes?   _____

Now, what is the real total … and what would an extra $300, or $400 or even $1000 a month mean to you?

ABOUT THE AUTHORS

Brig is one of the most successful Micro Entrepreneurs in the history of the Direct Selling Industry. He has produced multi billions in sales for the companies he has represented. He is an expert in training and educating professionals in the industry. Brig has been personally responsible for helping hundreds of people become millionaires, and influencing hundreds of thousands to enter the Micro Entrepreneurship workforce; where many earn thousands of dollars a month.

Bill Glynn is CEO of iSB Global Ventures. He has been a venture capitalist and entrepreneur for 20 years, and is the author of the best selling *Left on Red* and *The United States of Bankruptcy*. He was ranked by Information Week as one of 15 top innovators globally. He is a member of the *East West Institute's* President's Advisory Group, serving alongside distinguished government, industry and military leaders from across the world with a focus on critical issues such as the lack of potable water and food, natural resource scarcity, population growth, cyber security, warfare and chronic poverty.